I0106056

The true alchemists do not change lead into gold; they change the world into words.

-*William H. Gass*

ĬAM

CONTENTS

INDIE AUTHOR MAGAZINE

HELLO AND WELCOME!

I'm Indie Annie, and I'm thrilled you're reading this gorgeous full-color version of IAM. Did you know that you can also access all the information, education, and inspiration in our app? It's available on both the iOS App Store and Google Play. And for those that prefer to listen to me read articles, you can pop over to Spotify or our website. Happy Reading!

X

IndieAuthorMagazine.com

Download on the App Store

GET IT ON Google Play

Spotify

Don't Gamble with Your Author Career...

Go all in at the biggest indie author conference
November 8-12, 2021 Las Vegas, NV, USA

200+ presentations: Something for everyone at every point in your publishing journey

Industry day: Meet the distributors, service providers, and more!

Author signing day: Be a vendor, meet your favorite authors, and/or see how it's done by some of the best.

Plus: Many networking opportunities during the conference and after hours. Meet others in your genre or who share a special interest.

20 BOOKS TO 50K®

Join the 20Booksto50K® Facebook group for more info!

https://writelink.to/20Books

www.ingramcontent.com/pod-product-compliance
Lightning Source LLC
Chambersburg PA
CBHW080427030426
42335CB00020B/2623

From the Publisher

Magic and Alchemy.

As indie authors, our days are filled with the wonder of words and how they weave together to tell tales. Sometimes, reality can be a wondrous tale too. Let me tell you mine.

In 2017, I attended the Smarter Artist Summit in Austin, Texas. The conference was good, but what was exceptional was the connections made that day. Folks whose names are well-known in our little industry as solid authors, but whose generosity for sharing their journey up the author-preneur mountain has become legendary.

I was hooked. Being an indie author became my endgame. I had already published nonfiction for the travel industry. How hard could a pivot be to writing fiction?

I quickly learned. Writing fiction is hard. Publishing is harder.

Life went on. I dabbled, but mostly the day job kept me busy. The fever to crush it as a rapid-release bestselling indie author passed, but I stayed connected to the groups I had joined and kept learning.

Fast forward to 2019. My Scottish Clan MacDougall Gathering was announced for the end of July in Oban, Scotland. It was a promise kept to my Dad and Grandad before they passed away when I bought my ticket and made plans to travel solo. Coincidentally, the 20Booksto50K conference was announced in Edinburgh and the dates matched up to make a month-long Scottish adventure.

The dates coming together perfectly I credit to magic. Everything came together with such perfection that there's no other way for me to explain it.

But once 200 indie authors gathered in Edinburgh? Well, that's alchemy. The mixture of it all. The ingredients of the people and the place and what happened there defies reason and logic. I met people that have become more than best friends-they're family now. We write and travel together, and talk every day. We've written anthologies, created websites, celebrated launches, and started book clubs.

And now we've started a magazine.

We're from countries all over the world and write in different genres, but we're connected by our love of words and how we, as indie authors, share them with the world.

IAM isn't just a magazine. It's an extension of the community found online and in person. And if you're an indie author, or aspire to be one, it's your community too.

I plan to tell you more about the repeating pattern of magic and alchemy in our little community in my letters each month. For now, let me welcome you to our inaugural issue of Indie Author Magazine. It was born of the connections made at those two conferences (and now many others.) It's my hope that you'll find what our team found with one another. Magic and alchemy.

To your success,

Chelle

INDIE
AUTHOR MAGAZINE

PUBLISHER
Chelle Honiker

CREATIVE DIRECTOR
Alice Briggs

MANAGING EDITORS
Erika Everest
Robyn Sarty

STAFF WRITERS
Sìne Màiri MacDougall
Elaine Bateman
Laurel Decher
Chrishaun Keller Hanna
Marion Hermannsen
Anne Lown
Susan Odev

REGULAR CONTRIBUTORS
Patricia Carr
Ashli Faron
Fatima Fayez
Kasia Lasinska
Merri Maywether
Lasairiona McMaster
Clare Sager

PUBLISHER
Athenia Creative
6820 Apus Dr.
Sparks, NV, 89436 USA
775.298.1925

The publication, authors, and contributors reserve their rights in regards to copyright of their work. No part of this work covered by the copyright may be reproduced or copied in any form or by any means without the written consent of the publisher. All copyrighted work was reproduced with the permission of the owner.

Reasonable care is taken to ensure that *Indie Author Magazine* articles and other information on the website are up to date and as accurate as possible, at the time of publication, but no responsibility can be taken by *Indie Author Magazine* for any errors or omissions contained herein. Furthermore, *Indie Author Magazine* takes no responsibility for any losses, damages, or distress resulting from adherence to any information made available through this publication. The opinions expressed are those of the authors and do not necessarily reflect the views of *Indie Author Magazine*.

Cover Image by J Daniel Sawyer

From the Creative Director

This all started in a castle in Scotland…

There are times in your life when you make a quick decision, and it pays far richer dividends than you could ever imagine. My trip to Scotland became a cascade of adventures and blessings with a fabulous group of people I may have never known but for a quick thought: "Writing? Castle? Scotland? Sign me up!"

We hope to help you find similar serendipitous magic and alchemy throughout your writing career to lead to greater success than you would have found on your own, or at the very least accelerated success.

Whatever that looks like for you, because success looks like something, but it looks like something different for each of us.

Our goal is to give you something informative, accessible, and motivational within these pages no matter where you are on this journey, no matter what you write, no matter what choices you make to bring that vision of success to reality in your life. Those of us working on and for the magazine are at varying places on the authorial journey and write in a wide range of fiction and nonfiction. The variety of our interests will ensure you always find something useful here.

We welcome you as you join us on this journey. Pull up a chair, grab your favorite beverage, and sit with us for a chat or three. Then get up and conquer your mountain step by step.

Onward and Upward!

Alice Briggs
Creative Director,
Indie Author Magazine

From the Managing Editors

The part of indie publishing that makes my heart sing is not seeing my own words in print (although I like that too) but helping others to realize their publishing dreams. Indie Publishing has bypassed the traditional gatekeepers of literary agents and editors, but there are new gatekeepers in their placenow. Now, information is the key to the gate, and the lack of it is a barrier that can seem insurmountable.

When Chelle and Alice first floated the idea of a magazine for the indie author community, I knew I wanted to be part of it. When they presented the full scope of their vision, I realized that this was something really special. For me, it was the opportunity to give back to the community that has given me so much. To do it among friends I have made along the way? That's the icing on the cake.

In an industry that is growing and changing as rapidly as ours, current, reliable information is critical to making good decisions for your business. Collating and sharing that information to help authors help themselves is what drives us at *Indie Author Magazine*, and I feel privileged to be part of this unfolding story.

Let the magic begin.

Erika Everest
Managing Editor
Indie Author Magazine

The Start of Our Story

When Chelle Honiker and Alice Briggs first presented the notion of a magazine dedicated to the independent author community, I sat there like the little emoji with stars for eyes. I was enthralled. A magazine just for authors who treat their writing like a business? Yes please!

The first ereaders were launched in 1998, and the ability to self-publish followed soon after. The indie author community has grown exponentially since that time. And the one thing that continues to distinguish us from other industries is just that—we're a community. One that strives to support and help each other at every step of the way.

Here at *Indie Author Magazine*, we believe that we're just another extension of that community, and our goal is to serve our fellow authors.

This is our first issue, the start of our story, and our focus this month is outlining. Many stories start with an outline and grow from there. So too is our hope that this magazine will grow and develop. And with you as part of our community, I believe it will.

Robyn Sarty
Managing Editor,
Indie Author Magazine

Why a Magazine?

One of the best things about the indie author community is that it is first and foremost a community. It's unique because in the strictest sense, we aren't competing with one another. We can collaborate and satisfy the needs of our readers through the power of cooperation. A rising tide truly does raise all boats.

Because we're wired to tell stories about flawed characters and redemption, we understand empathy and that makes us one of the most diverse and inclusive communities many of us have been a part of. We're constantly helping one another, sharing resources, tips, tools, and ideas to try.

On social media and at conferences, it never seems to matter who is sitting beside you or what they write, there is an instant connection because you're both writers. The differences make us unique, but they do not divide because we have such a strong common activity. Conversation and celebration can, and do, last for years..

Online groups are useful, and allow for quick responses to issues or questions, but then posts get buried. Conferences are fabulous for more in-depth discussions and learning, but most are only once per year, and can be expensive to get to. We love both of these opportunities, but we wanted more.

Thus, the idea for *Indie Author Magazine* began. We searched, but didn't find any that were offered in multiple formats and that focused on the unique challenges that indie authors face at whatever stage of their career. We found conflicting and biased information, and it was hard to sift through what worked and what was hype, or presented with the intent to sell a product, service, or course.

We wanted unbiased, well-researched information, with context and sources we could trust.

In this gap, we believe we can be a bridge between the immediacy of online groups and the depth of conferences, and be an additional source of community building for all of us in this space.

Our goal is for IAM to be the source for solid information you can trust. We'll do that by covering topics common to indie authors, often presenting multiple viewpoints, but with context. We'll refrain from being prescriptive. We'll celebrate successes and support you in times of pivoting when plans go awry.

Everyone at IAM is a working indie author. We come from different countries. Different genres. Different stages of our career. But what binds us together is that we're a community. And so, IAM isn't really something foreign and untested. It's simply an extension of an existing community, and you're very welcome here. ◼

Dear Indie Annie,

I've been working on my story for a while now, and at first I really loved it. Lately though, I'm starting to wonder if it's any good. I know I'll need an editor, but should I just give up on it? How do I know if my story is worth finishing?

Thanks,
Conflicted in Calgary

DEAR CONFLICTED,

We are rarely the best judges of our own work, especially when we have been living with it for a while. Having doubts about your story, or your abilities as a writer, is perfectly normal. I doubt there is a writer on the planet, or through history, who hasn't sat where you are now, facing their precious manuscript, and wanting to throw it all in the recycling bin. Impostor syndrome is rife in the writing community, and I would dare to say it is even more acute in the indie publishing world because we don't have the comforting validation of a publisher who says they believe in our story and our talent.

An editor's job is to make your words shine. They work with you to bring your vision to light. A developmental editor will help you ensure consistency and deal with any plot holes or problems in your timeline or characterization. A line editor or proofreader is there to fix your grammar, syntax, and typos. They may have views on how good your story is, but even if they are avid readers in your genre, that is not their job. A good editor will keep those views to themselves.

You could find yourself a critique partner. Many writers belong to creative writing groups, and these can be useful sources of feedback on your work, but if they don't read in your genre, their opinions may be of limited value. And if they do write in your genre, think as well about their experience. What makes them qualified to offer their opinion? Are they successfully publishing in your field? Are they also Indies?

Need help from your favorite Indie Aunt?
Ask Dear Indie Annie a question at
IndieAnnie@indieauthormagazine.com

In reality, the only people qualified to decide if your story is any good are your readers. It is much better to ask for feedback from the people who are most likely to buy your book.

I would suggest joining groups/discussion boards run by readers in your genre. There are many groups like this on Goodreads and Facebook. If you are a fan of the genre you are writing in (and if not, why are you writing this at all?) then you are probably already a member of some of these groups. Reach out to their members and ask for volunteers to beta read for you.

Be honest, tell them you are a new author and that this is still a WIP (work in progress). Many will jump at the chance to help you craft your tale.

One word of caution, though, from your Indie Aunt, be careful not to worry too much about the views of one person. Everyone has their own opinions and can hold them quite forcefully, but they are only their opinions. If several people tell you the same thing, then you may have a problem with the story that needs to be addressed.

Remember, this is your story. Your world, your characters, your vision. Your baby. Writing is a bit like being a parent. You start out full of hope for this new life and over time you doubt you are doing anything right. The ultimate test of your success is to send that child out into the world.

So, finish your book, ask for feedback, edit and publish.

Happy writing,
Indie Annie X

10 TIPS FOR #INSTAGRAM

U sed correctly, Instagram is a powerful tool that can help elevate your career. There are many ways for you to optimize your Instagram as an author. Here, we provide the top ten tips to help you bring your Instagram A-game to the #bookstagram and #authorsofinstagram community. The ultimate tip, however, is also my favorite: don't forget to have fun!

1 OPTIMIZE YOUR BIO

The "name" section in your Instagram bio is the only searchable part of your profile (other than your username), so use it well!

Pro Tip: Include your genre and the fact that you're an author, as well as your full name, in the "name" section. These are keywords and therefore valuable Instagram bio real estate. For example, you could use: *"Mary Poppins | Thriller Author".*

In the text of your bio, let users know why they should follow you, and what they can expect from you if they do.

For example:
Follow for cozy bookish photos and book-related recipes.
Join me for behind the scenes glimpses into the life of a thriller author.

The last line of your bio should be a call to action (CTA) and relate directly to your link.

For instance:
Grab my free short story by signing up to my newsletter ⬇
https://marypoppinsauthor.com/subscribe

2 AESTHETICS

Your profile picture should be a photo of you, or a likeness of you. Instagram is a visual platform, and its users are as well. They want to connect with you. If you're using an anonymous pen name, consider using a cartoon likeness or silhouette photo of you, rather than just a picture of a book or a journal. Readers are keen to get to know the person behind the words they love, and using a profile picture that lets them put a face to a name is half the battle.

How does your profile and Instagram "grid" look taken together? Is it uniform? Does it form a cohesive whole? Instagram users tend to take a quick glance at your profile and decide in a split second whether to follow.

Pro Tip: Declutter your profile with a single click: you can hide photos from your grid without deleting them by using the "archive" function. The photos are still there, but now visible only to you.

3 THEME

You can switch up the look and feel of your profile by using "themes". Creating a theme is as simple as using the same prop or background for all of your photos. Done well, it makes your photos instantly recognizable and forms part of your brand. You can change your theme as you like: depending on the season, the month, or even your mood. For example, summertime could feature green tones and plants, while October could be pumpkins.

Pro Tip: Integrate your own books into your Instagram "theme". That way, you will position your books alongside any other book you post about (both traditionally and indie published).

4 CAPTIONS

The Instagram algorithm loves to see engagement. If you can show that users want to engage with your content, it sends a message that the content is valuable and will potentially be shown more.

The simplest way to drive engagement is through asking questions in captions. Bookish questions perform especially well on bookstagram, where many users use the initials "QOTD" (Question of the Day). For example: "Who is your favorite character of all time and why?" Don't forget to answer your own question. Readers will be naturally curious, and your answer could spark further discussion in the comments.

Your QOTD does not have to relate to your photo, but it helps when it does. You can also use the caption as a space to update readers on what's going on in your life, or what you're currently working on.

7 GENUINE ENGAGEMENT IS KING

Do not follow accounts and then unfollow them once they follow you back — it creates bad rapport. Follow the accounts you genuinely have an interest in and engage with them. Like their photos, answer their QOTD, and write comments. Bookstagram is a lovely community, but you have to be willing to fully participate and give back.

Pro Tip: Giveaways can increase your following and engagement. They can also foster a sense of community and bring you closer to your readers. The giveaway doesn't need to be your own book, but ensure it is genre appropriate. The key is moderation — you want to attract quality followers who will stay for you and your content, not freebie seekers.

5 HASHTAGS

Research is an important part of any successful marketing strategy, and Instagram is no different. To make sure that your posts are seen by the largest pool of readers, use both niche hashtags (such as #booksandcoffeeplease) and broader hashtags (#books, #bookstagrammer).

Pro Tip: Create your own hashtag using your author name. Readers tend to hashtag author names. If the hashtag exists, they are likely to use it when talking about your books in their own posts.

Another tip is to max out your hashtags. Instagram allows you to use up to thirty hashtags – use them all. The more you use, the greater the chance that someone browsing through the hashtag will find your account.

Pro Tip: You can follow your favorite hashtags. They'll appear on your "following" page just like normal user accounts.

6 HARD COPIES WORK BEST

Using paperbacks or hardbacks results in the most aesthetically pleasing photos. While many bookstagram users read traditionally published books, it doesn't mean they don't read indie. Invest in author copies and take pictures of them, as well as other books in your genre.

8 DO NOT SELF-PROMO AND RUN

Accounts where every photo is a promo graphic created on BookBrush or Canva won't get traction. Instagram users, like all readers, want value, and not spammy graphics. Incorporate posts about your books among posts about other similar books or your writing process.

Pro Tip: Instead of using traditional promo graphics, consider taking photos of your book or your Kindle. You can still inform readers where your book is available in the caption.

> Writing is easy.
> All you have to do is cross out the wrong words.
> -Mark Twain

(9) KNOW YOUR AUDIENCE

Find your audience and cater to them. If you write fiction, your audience is readers – "bookstagrammers". You can post about your favorite books and books similar to yours. You can talk about themes, tropes or even covers.

If you write non-fiction for authors then your target audience is other authors. You can post writing tips and talk about craft. Of course, other authors are also readers, but you want to prime your audience toward your primary product. It's difficult to have an account focused solely on writing tips and expect your fiction book to sell on release day.

(10) INSTAGRAM STORIES

Use Instagram Stories to create quick content. The photos you snap for stories don't have to be perfect — stories disappear in 24 hours. Use Instagram's embedded engagement tools in your stories: create simple polls or ask questions. Repost your readers' answers and comment on them, creating another avenue for discussion.

Pro Tip: Create a "Welcome" or "Start here!" story that will enable new readers to easily learn about you and your books, and add it to "highlights." Unlike regular stories, highlights stay on your profile until you delete them. Create a custom cover image for your highlight that complements your overall brand. ∎

Kasia Lasinska

Podcasts We Love

THE AUTHOR ARENA

Hosted by Fatima Fayez, Merri Maywether, Paddy Finn

Three authors from three different genres come together to share the tools indie authors use in the self-publishing arena.

https://writelink.to/j56uih

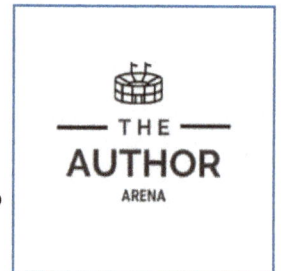

WISH I'D KNOWN THEN...

Hosted by Jami Albright and Sara Rosett

Being an indie author is more than knowing the latest marketing trend, it's about being innovative and creative and learning from your mistakes.

https://writelink.to/u99ipe

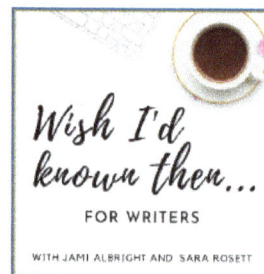

THE CREATIVE PENN

Hosted by Joanna Penn

A weekly podcast that includes interviews, inspiration, and information on writing and creativity, publishing options, book marketing, and creative entrepreneurship.

https://writelink.to/jdq4me

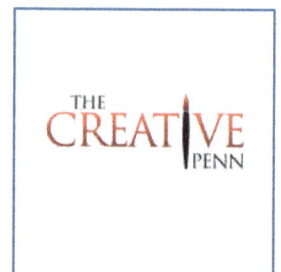

Outlining Puzzle

Find the Following Outlining Words in the Puzzle

```
Y E N R U O J S E N I O R E H
B U I L D I N G B L O C K S N
T C E T I H C R A R K P L H Y
I T E R A T I V E T A R E T D
M L E P S M N N S N Y R O T S
Y I N K R T N O T T O T Z V Y
R E S W A A R S T S C G R R L
E O T B L L E U J E A A E Z L
V U F P E R F O C R L T X S J
O T A D M L U W D T T E T M K
C L R B D R I E O O U A K R J
S I D P N Y N E L N E R J S L
I N J E M E T P F B S L E M R
D E Y G R V M Z T D M B M X T
```

Skeleton	Misbelief
Outline	Lie
Heros Joourney	Story
Plotter	Discovery
Pantser	Architect
Beats	Gardener
Draft	Acts
Planner	Structuree
Iterative	Building Blocks
Snowflake	

GAIL CARRIGER

As someone who has received her share of accolades and recognition over the years in traditional publishing, Gail realizes the lessons she absorbed served her well as an indie author.

Gail Carriger writes great heroines. With thirteen *New York Times* bestsellers, over a million books in print, and her Parasol Protectorate Series optioned for animation, it was a natural fit for Gail to write and independently publish her latest book *The Heroine's Journey* for writers, readers, and fans of pop culture.

Gail identifies as a hybrid author — an author that is both traditionally and independently published. There are many benefits of being a hybrid. Gail shares, "I started out traditional and have moved towards self-publishing over the last decade. Trad helped me build a great platform and gave me experience doing things that most strictly indie authors don't get, like: book tours, school visits, large industry events, magazine ads, music videos, merch vendors, and so forth (not that we can't organize such things for ourselves now, I'm just not sure I would bother). Traditional has the reach, particularly in the YA sphere with schools, libraries, bookstores, and Hollywood that I either can't access or is too much work for my lazy soul."

As someone who has received her share of accolades and recognition over the years in traditional publishing, Gail realizes the lessons she absorbed served her well as an indie author. More specifically she says she learned, "A lot about marketing — what works on a large scale and what doesn't, what depends on the author and what depends on the publisher, what's easy for one person to do, and what requires a team. I also learned a lot about cover art techniques,

Image by Vanessa Applegate

Featured Author

Being a hybrid she has the best of both worlds, as she confirms, "I've never been an 'all my eggs in one basket' kind of person, so this approach to a career is very satisfying for me."

publicity campaigns, IP ownership, legal protections, outsourcing to experts, that sort of thing. But I think my best lesson was in how to relate to big businesses, whether it's a large publishing conglomerate or Amazon, it's better not to take things they do personally. No matter which side of the equation I choose (trad or indie), as an author, all the large corporations I work with really care about is their bottom line. They do not care about me as an author or my book. This is not unfair, this is business. The most important thing any author can do is write a good book. The second most important thing is protect themselves by thinking about that book as a product and themselves as a business, because everyone else will."

She explains, "These days I also benefit as a hybrid author from working with smaller presses and indie artists to produce beautiful hardcovers and fancy tie-in projects that specifically satisfy fans who collect printed books as art." Being a hybrid she has the best of both worlds, as she confirms, "I've never been an 'all my eggs in one basket' kind of person, so this approach to a career is very satisfying for me. As I'm fond of saying, "I diversify my assets. Why wouldn't I diversify my writing business?" Also I kind of love being able to do The Thing on a whim."

In this case, *The Thing* became *The Heroine's Journey*. As many authors have come to recognize, sometimes there's no better person to write the book you want to read than yourself. Gail was inspired to write *The Heroine's Journey* because no one had written it. She shares, "All those conventions I attended over the years had so many conversations and panels about the hero's journey, but I have a background in classics and I studied the heroine's journey as an undergraduate. So I was constantly saying, 'okay yeah, but in the heroine's journey...' and getting BLANK looks.

> A common theme in *The Heroine's Journey* is that of belonging. As an indie author focused on the author-business perspective, it would be an asset to capitalize on this.

Then someone would ask, 'So is there a book on the heroine's journey? Like for storytellers?' And I would have to say, 'Erm, no, not really.' Because there are books but they tend to be Jungian psyche orientated. So finally, after waiting for someone else to write it, I figured it was my job until someone better came along."

It's challenging to imagine who that someone better could be. *The Heroine's Journey* outlines the basic structure, beats, themes, and messages, and if applied suitably authors will be rewarded with a loyal readership. Among the many gems from the book, Gail hopes authors reading *The Heroine's Journey* learn, "A step-by-step breakdown of how to successfully write this journey, and an understanding of how it is different from the hero's. An ability to identify it in film, literature, and more. A desire to question why we prioritise, emphasise, and discuss the hero's journey while vilifying the heroine's and how this has impacted most aspects of pop culture from the dialogue around what is "worthy" to how we distribute accolades and recognition."

A common theme in *The Heroine's Journey* is that of belonging. As an indie author focused on the author-business perspective, it would be an asset to capitalize on this. There are several ways authors can add an element of belonging to their books to deepen readers' connections to the book and series. Gail offers this tip, "Side characters are fantastic for this. Appealing, vibrant, complex, varied, and supportive side characters allow different readers to see themselves or someone they love as one of those characters. Readers want to fall in love with your characters, so give them a range of things to love about them and identify with."

Indeed, Gail has plenty of valuable advice for new authors on building reader relationships. She says, "Treat your readers exactly how you would want your favorite author to treat you. If you are on social media as your author self then you are there for your readers, not for yourself. Give them what they want, and if you don't know what that is, you don't know your own brand or books very well, because that is what they want. You will get the same question a million times from different readers, remember that for them it's the first time they've ever asked it, and for some of them it's the first time they've reached out to any author. It is the hardest thing to lead with compassion but also the most rewarding. And if you can't think of anything to say, remember they took the time to reach out to you, so 'thank you' works wonders. On a simpler note? See how indie romance authors are doing it, they are unquestionably the BEST in the business at building reader relationships."

With the turmoil of 2020, many conventions were postponed or cancelled. When asked how the pandemic changed her relationship with readers, Gail shared, "I feel oddly closer to them; since I haven't been able to do events many of them have reached out via email or my newsletter or in my Facebook fan group. It's actually become easier for them, in a way, to ping me and say how much something I wrote uplifted their spirits. A few have asked for personal notes due to loss or for a depressed family member. I've tried to stay up-beat and positive as much as I can, since I feel like comfort is part of my role and responsibility to them, having had their unflagging

> # "Be kind to yourself and to others.
> ## *Support. Solidarity. Comfort.*
> "

support for so long. Since I have met so many of them in-person over the years it feels necessary to both of us to stay accessible."

The world is slowly opening back up, with author and reader conventions being scheduled over the coming months. After a year of isolation, many readers are eager to reconnect and conventions will be active again. Gail has several favorites and recommends, "I have a ton that I love. I try to go to smaller fan run conventions, industry only gatherings, book fairs, something international, and at least one Comic Con. They each have different things to recommend them. I'm a social author — still an introvert but I genuinely like hanging out with other authors and with my readers. I get more of a chance to meet readers at small cons, but I see more friends inside the industry at larger events. Many of my author friends go to World Con or World Fantasy so I try to make at least one of those each year. Also, I really like traveling and an author event is a great excuse to see a new place."

In the meantime, while we wait for the world to open up to meet again, Gail offers these last words to authors, echoed from *The Heroine's Journey*, "Be kind to yourself and to others. Support. Solidarity. Comfort."

You can read more about Gail Carriger on her website: https://writelink.to/rwdnut

■   Fatima Fayez

Neither a Plotter Nor a Pantser Be

THE BENEFITS OF OUTLINING

If you stand at the front of a conference room full of authors and ask for a show of hands who are "pantsers" and who are "plotters," you would start a literary battle, possibly literally. Feelings run high in both camps. The question for any indie author is, will one method prove to be more efficient for me than the other?

Indie authors trade in words already written. There is no publisher's advance to fill the fridge and stock your cupboards. The key to success is to get your story out there as quickly as possible. If there is a way to ensure optimum efficiency whilst maintaining quality control that allows you enough creative freedom to keep the artist inside sated, then surely that's the winning ticket. Many successful authors cite outlining as the cleverest way forward.

Before looking at what outlining is and how it potentially is a meeting point between the two styles, let's explore what we mean by pantsing and plotting. Pantsers, a.k.a. discovery writers, say that they do not plan their writing in advance; they prefer to let the story unfold. Plotters, on the other hand, cannot put pen to paper, finger to keyboard, or even voice to dictaphone without knowing all the details of their story before they begin.

> "Pantsing is flying by the seat of your pants or going with the flow"

Indie author, Libbie Hawker, in her influential work *Take Off Your Pants!*, describes pantsing as "flying by the seat of your pants; going with the flow." She is very clear that if she could habitually "pants" fast enough to support her career, she would "wear party hats all day long and do a happy-dance every time..." However, she states that "if your goals include quitting your day job... then effective outlining is a skill you must learn."

She advocates a three-legged outline method that builds a Story Core, namely establishing three key aspects:

> "Plot is a sequence of events, the action that goes on outside of the character."

Character Arc
Theme and
Pacing

Hawker maintains that this approach differs from plotting every detail. For her, "plot is a sequence of events, the action that goes on outside of the character." Though plot can form the additional leg to your stool and help to provide the structure of your story with greater strength and integrity, breaking things down into that level of detail is unnecessary if you have the other three legs in place. She argues she can outline a novel in half a day. Time well invested, as it allows you to write faster, with no dead ends, fewer plot holes and still provides the writer with the freedom to channel their muse.

USA Today bestselling author, Dean Wesley Smith, who has published over a hundred books in his long career, argues the opposite. He is clear that any form of outlining is the death of creativity. In his book, *Writing into the Dark*, he extolls the joy of unleashing the creative voice and parks outlining firmly with the critical voice. "Great art is rarely, if ever, created from a critical perspective." Writing into the dark forges the same energy for writers as being lost in a story has for a reader. The creative voice "is telling the story and entertaining us as we type." Dean advocates actively turning off the critique in your head. To prepare for "writing into the dark," read freely and with joyful abandon. "... If you automatically copy-edit everything you read, go get help. And I mean real help. Professional help, because you have lost all ability to see a story and are trapped by the little black marks on the paper." A very strong viewpoint, but Dean admits he does outline, after the creative voice has said its piece. At the end of each chapter, he stops and thinks about what happened. He outlines in reverse to capture plot points as he writes, and then loops back to edit and address any plot holes.

> Writing into the dark forges the same energy for writers as being lost in a story has for a reader.

A third way to explore the process is to think of outlining as "plot gardening," as described in Chris Fox's book of the same name. Fox is a well-established indie author with an extremely popular YouTube channel, *ChrisFoxWrites*, and his "plantsing" idea likens the writer's occupation to that of a gardener. He divides the world into two types. Architects, authors who plan every minute detail and discovery writers who put the seeds of the story on the ground and wait to discover what comes out. Chris argues it is folly to leave the garden unattended, but too much control can also stifle growth. The writer should act as a gardener. You plant the seeds and nurture them, guide them, train them into your novel. The metaphor extends across the book. From planting seeds (characters/world-building) to adding guide poles (following a structure such as Dan Harmon's Story Circle or the Save the Cat beats—focusing on the beats and laying out the scenes) to tending your garden (plot branching, cultivating characters, planning the next harvest) and enriching the soil (reading/watching content to inspire and inform the story).

These three experienced and successful fiction and non-fiction authors, though their perspectives may differ, agree that however you approach your writing you must let the book breathe. Though most of us would struggle to let go of the reins as Dean Wesley Smith urges, his argument that both the critical and creative voice cannot happily coexist is difficult to refute. Chris Fox and Libbie Hawker recognize this challenge, and their hybrid methods aim to harness the best of both worlds. Neither pure plotters nor pantsers, they use structures to provide a framework from which to write smarter.

For non-fiction books, arguably, there is an even greater need to harness the critical voice. You need to qualify your statements, prove your research, and arrange your chapters and subsections logically to scaffold the reader's understanding. Outlining is not about over-analyzing or becoming paralysed in the detail. There are no hard and fast rules. If a structure helps you write faster, whilst still allowing your creative voice its freedom, then that's the sweet spot. In their books, these writers explore their methods to manage and maintain the creative process with maximum business efficiency, but what works for them might not work for you.

Finding what works for you is the key, and there are many systems to choose from. Check out this comprehensive list of twelve outlining methods to help you find one that works for you. Alternatively, take a look at Prowriting Aid's suggestions which show you can work equally well with old school index cards or modern-day programs like Trello.

The title of this article is a play on Polonius's words in Shakespeare's Hamlet (Act I, Sc. III). The quote runs, "Neither a borrower nor a lender be..." Polonius warns of the need to avoid extremes and temper your decisions with the wisdom of the middle ground, but above all be honest with yourself. Outlining should help you write better books, faster. But if you rail against it and want to write free, then that's what is best for you, and if you prefer more structure, detail every plotline in advance. But whatever you do, as Polonius says, "To thine ownself be true." ■

Susan Odev

Outlining the Problem:

Many authors begin their outlining process by developing entire character profiles as well as the basic idea of what will happen in the book. They feel they at least need to know where they're going to take their reader, what the reader is going to expect of the story, and how they plan on meeting those expectations while still telling the story they want to tell. Sounds complicated, doesn't it?

These authors suggest that you begin with a story arc: the overall shape of the story or the rise and fall of tension or emotion where readers get to see the cause-and-effect connections between what appears to be otherwise random occurrences.

Then it comes down to writing strong characters with clear motivation from the get-go. As human beings we are conditioned to avoid conflict. But as readers, we live for it, we expect to feel all the things, all the time. You could try to argue against this, but consider this: if you picked up a book from the library with a blacked out cover not knowing what lay within, and the story ended up being about a guy and a girl who were happy all the time and nothing ever went wrong in their lives. They lived their best life one hundred percent of the time and got everything they've always dreamed of having. Boring book, right? That book would likely get a huge "DNF" stamped across it, right? And you'd move onto something with more depth, more *conflict*. Why? Because conflict is the soul of a great book.

A good book needs conflict, it's true, but what good is conflict if you don't have a relatable character to cheer for, or against? Characters and their motivations are key for producing a gratifying *story*.

An enjoyable story will trump great writing every day of the week. All the technically accurate writing in the world won't garner you super-fans if you don't have a compelling story with strong characters dragging them along for the ride.

Lisa Cron (*Story Genius*) says as readers we expect the protagonist will:

- Be vulnerable
- Have a past
- Want something
- Have a defining misbelief
- Struggle to make sense of everything
- Make the problem worse with everything they do.

Essentially your main character will have something they need to do (goal), a problem within themselves (misbelief),

Conflict and Misbeliefs

and a problem in their world they need to overcome (conflict).

So what is a misbelief?

Misbeliefs are false thoughts your character believes about themselves. They're not actually true, in fact, often, the only person who actually believes the misbelief is the character themselves. They tend to be "I am" statements. For example: "I am not enough," "I am unlovable," "I am weak," or "I am a terrible decision maker." Once you pick a misbelief for your character, you need to establish at what point in their life this misbelief was born, and why or what happened in their life to make them believe this false thing about themselves?

Perhaps your character is a terrible decision maker because she lived a sheltered life with overprotective parents who made all their decisions for her. Perhaps your character pushes away love as a grown-up because he couldn't get his busy parents to pay him any attention as a child and he feels something about his very being is unloveable. Match the symptom to the cause.

So you've got your misbelief, and your root cause of why your character feels this way about themselves, now what do you do with this information?

Have fun with it. Create a broken character and stick them front and center, wearing their brokenness like a beacon.

If your character believes she's a terrible decision maker—throw a bunch of decisions at her. For a while she's going to make everything worse, right? She's going to believe more and more that she's a terrible decision maker because you're going to make all of her decisions hit her in her misbelief.

If your character believes he's unloveable——throw in a character who falls in love with him.

The plot you write forces the character to stare their misbelief down in an epic battle of self. Along their journey, there will be various points where they feel as though they are winning the battle and then *bam* you will come and smack them back down into the pit of self-loathing. This is usually until their ally (friend or foe) kicks them in the rear, forces them to see their misbelief under a spotlight, and realize it's untrue. Their whole life since the point of embracing their misbelief has been, in many ways, a lie.

From the moment you begin your outline or write those first words of your novel, the character's misbelief is right there, whispering in their ear about how

they are. This is how you get your readers to relate to your story, because as human beings, we all believe we are somehow flawed, and reading about other people's flaws make us feel as though we aren't alone.

This process works for antagonists and antiheros as well as the protagonist. In fact, a strong misbelief in your main antagonist can do wonders for a story. If your bad guy's misbelief is "I am alone," something happened to him throughout his life to make him believe he needs to stay alone. But he meets a beautiful woman in a coffee shop that he's intrigued by and wants to spend time with. He's immediately in conflict with himself. His misbelief is screaming at him to push her away, while part of him wants to take the risk and talk to her.

Tying every step of your novel back to a character's misbelief will ensure your story remains logical and flows in a way the reader can connect to. How would a person who believes their

decisions are all terrible react when faced with decisions? Would that change based on the magnitude of the decision? How would they feel when they make a decision, and it goes as poorly as they expect? All of these nuances of your characters psyche will influence your decisions throughout the book as the author. Do you want someone to make decisions for her? What effect would that have?

For a strong story, start your outlining process with:

1. Your story, at the very least know where you want it to go
2. Create your characters
3. Find a misbelief that works with those plot points

If you get stuck, loop back to the character's misbelief, figure out how they would react to the situation and remember why they react the way they do. It will bring a depth to your writing, and make everything a little more logical along the way. ■

Lasairiona McMaster

A LOOK AT ADVANCED OUTLINING METHODS FOR PLOTTERS AND PANTSERS

L et's look at two representative methods for plotters and pantsers: the Snowflake Method and the Skeleton Draft.

To lead us into the discussion, we'll briefly touch on the topic of beat iterations. This is an important concept that will help you to be a better drafter, whether you plan your outline meticulously, or whether you prefer to sit down and let the muse inspire you.

ITERATIVE BEATS

Beats are the small components of scenes. For example, if you write a scene about a car accident, the beats might be: driver is driving along, chatting to the passenger. They argue, and the driver is distracted. They crash into the car ahead, and the passenger bangs their head because they weren't buckled in. The driver calls an ambulance, feeling guilty and scared. The other car driver berates them. And on and on. Each sentence is a beat.

Beats can be part of a plotter's chapter and scene structure and are extremely flexible. You can plan out the beat for each scene of each chapter before ever writing a single word of your first draft.

Or you can sketch out beats roughly before writing each scene which might suit pantsers. It's entirely up to you. There's no wrong or right way.

THE SNOWFLAKE METHOD

Developed by writer Randy Ingermanson, the Snowflake Method focuses on adding ever more intricate layers in the same way a snowflake grows from the inside out.

1. **In Step One**, you capture your plot idea in a one-sentence summary which might include your genre, the protagonist, and the stakes.

Summarizing your own story may be one of the most difficult tasks for writers. Knocking off one hundred thousand words of a first draft seems easy compared to condensing an entire book into one sentence.

That's why starting an outline with the absolute essence of your plot is such a great idea. You're not too close to the story yet, and the one-sentence summary can guide you throughout the entire planning process.

> The Snowflake Method focuses on adding ever more intricate layers in the same way a snowflake grows from the inside out

2. **Step Two** expands the one-sentence summary into one paragraph. Ingermanson suggests following the Three Disaster structure to determine setup, one sentence each for the three disasters to befall your protagonist, and one sentence for the ending. The second disaster prevents the "saggy middle" problem.

3. **Step Three** looks at characters. Repeat Steps One and Two for each main character's personal story. You might also look at their motivations, goals, conflict, and epiphanies.

4. **Step Four** expands each sentence of the one-paragraph summary into its own paragraph to create a full page summary. This forces you to flesh out your initial ideas with more detail.

5. In **Step Five**, you'll create a full page description for each character. Tell the story from their point of view. This is going to be invaluable when you weave their progress into your plot outline.

6. You're now at **Step Six** where you make the big, bold decisions. Expand each paragraph from your one-page summary to a full page. You should be left with a four to five page synopsis. It's perfectly fine to go over your previous work and change details. This is a flexible work in progress, not set in stone.

7. In **Step Seven**, Ingermanson suggests you deepen your characters by working out their history, motivation, their foibles, their likes and dislikes. This can take up several pages per character.

8. In **Steps Eight and Nine**, you dig even deeper. Make a list of key scenes and add a paragraph synopsis, including settings, goal, and conflict.

And finally, you're ready to type your first draft. You have enough information to move from scene to scene easily while there's plenty of space to add subplots and find lovely surprises your characters kept from you.

SKELETON DRAFT

While the Snowflake Method works best for plotters, Steff Green's *Skeleton Draft* is a great tool for pantsers, or gardeners, as she calls herself. Steff is an award-winning author in the Reverse Harem genre and, under her pen name Steffanie Holmes, writes a book in six weeks, using this method.

Before she begins drafting, she works out a main character, a hook to pull the reader in right from the start, a conflict, what genre she wants to write in, and how she wants her novel to end.

Then she writes her scenes, laying down lines of dialog, bits of plot, and whatever else she feels might happen in a particular scene.

When she's done, she has a pre-draft so rough, she says it's laughable. Yet this is how she begins every novel. Despite the sketchy treatment, she is able to use large chunks in her finished novel, so very little of her time is wasted.

We had the pleasure of putting some questions to Steff.

> We discover the story while we write it.

How long does your process take?

Most of my books come in at 90k plus. I have a six weeks writing process: three days for the skeleton draft, two to three weeks for the first and second draft. Three weeks for the final draft.

I've been using this method for over fifty books. I do struggle with continuity errors and tend to forget people's names or eye colors. As my process develops, I'm getting better at it. Plus I have a team of beta readers and editors.

Were you surprised by the reception of skeleton draft?

Yes, I really was. The skeleton draft was supposed to be a bonus for a bigger course. It's the most popular non-fiction thing I've ever done.

How does your method differ from creating a scene summary outline?

The idea of writing a synopsis or making a spreadsheet makes me go "bleah." I get halfway through the outline and say to myself, "I don't want to write the book now. I already know what's going to happen." It just isn't exciting any more.

When I started skeleton-drafting, I thought everyone wrote their books that way. Even if they started with an outline, I assumed they'd then move on to skeleton drafting. It was only in the last few years, I realized that no, that's a weird thing to do.

Here is why skeleton-drafting is different: when you sit down over three days and pour out the story, you're giving yourself an outline that's part of the story. Every word goes towards the final word count. If I did a traditional summary outline, I might have 2-5k words. With my

allows me to get through the plot stuff that has to happen while I get to know my characters organically.

Outliners often have the problem that their books are plot heavy. Their characters might feel wooden and two-dimensional because they aren't in their characters' heads. Whereas gardeners focus on their characters but may get lost in the plot. I combine the best of both methods.

Thanks for your time, Steff!

If you'd like to learn more, Steff Green explains her method in detail on her podcast "Rage Against the Manuscript" as well as in her course "Writing Your Skeleton Draft." ■

Marion Hermannsen

method, I have 10-20k words that go towards the final book. Nothing is wasted.

Indie authors write fast, so that appealed to me. Often, we gardners are told we need to learn to outline to write faster. Actually, if you really can't stand outlining, try skeleton-drafting. It's an outline that works to our strengths. We discover the story while we write it.

I found a second strength in this approach. Generally, I have an idea about a character when I start, but I don't know them well until halfway through the book. If I were a plotter, I'd write character bios and description. Using my method, I'm not wasting time at the beginning, planning these characters. Skeleton-drafting

LOST THE PLOT?
WE GOT YOU COVERED!

You've decided to write that novel. You opened Word, but now you're staring at a blank screen and… what? What actually goes into writing a novel?

This is when Plottr walks in wearing a poncho, chewing a cigar, and it's here to be your hero.

Plottr is a visual outlining tool for writers, developed by YA author Cameron Sutter and aspiring author Ryan Zee.

GETTING STARTED

Whether you're a plotter who refuses to start your novel without ten thousand words of outline, or a discovery writer (pantser) who just starts typing with little to no direction in mind,

Plottr can help. You can use it to plot ahead, keep track of the plot, characters and settings as you write, or organize what you've already written (did the guy in chapter two fire five bullets or six?)

HOW YOU USE IT IS UP TO YOU.

The Visual Timeline consists of rows headed by chapters and columns showing plot lines. Each scene card within the timeline is similar to a digital index card or post-it note on a wall.

Scene cards can be edited with plot, scene, and character comments, and can be moved around the timeline or added to. So, if your character goes to grab the gun in chapter ten, and you realize you forgot to put it in the drawer in chapter three, just nip back and add it in.

Learning a new system can feel overwhelming. We asked the guys over at Plottr what advice they would give to anyone considering the app. Troy Lambert, Plottr's Education Lead and a Mystery/Thriller author, suggests "If you're new to Plottr, start simply by creating scene cards to get your ideas down and add a couple plot lines and chapters to get a feel for how the software works."

> Each scene card within the timeline is similar to a digital index card or post-it note on a wall.

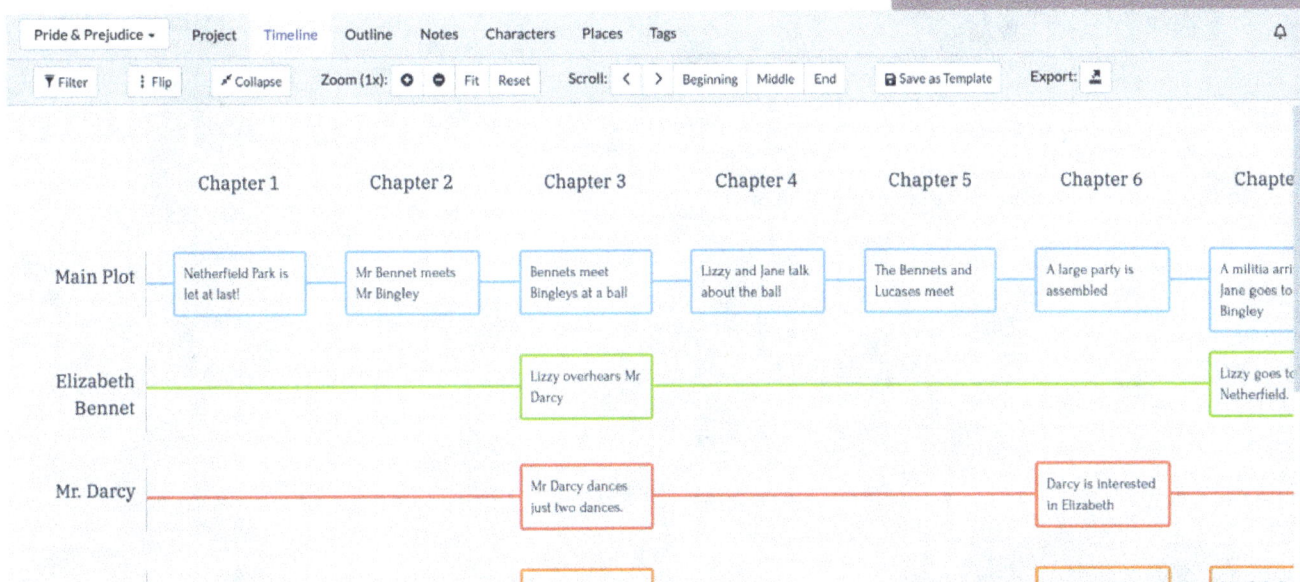

Screenshot from Plottr Demo, showing two characters and how they connect to the main plot for Pride and Prejudice.

Still facing that white screen? Plottr provides beat templates to help you navigate the ups and downs of a story. You can follow The Hero's Journey, Romancing the Beat, or the Twelve Chapter Mystery, to name but a few. Each box in the timeline opens up to give an example of what you could enter into that chapter.

Sci-Fi and Fantasy indie powerhouse, Michael Anderle, Founder and CEO of LMBPN Publishing, confirmed that Plottr is the main program he uses to create new concepts. "What I like is the ability to get the job done of laying out beats and easily change my mind. It has the functionality that I want, while allowing me to add more details should I desire."

LEVELING UP

"As you start dipping your toes deeper, try using custom attributes for scenes, characters, and places, which will help you think of new

PRO-TIP

Include additional plotlines called "Questions" and "Answers" and use them to track the loops you open in each chapter (questions) and when you close them later (answers). If you number them, a quick scan of your plot lines will identify if there are any loops still open that you need to close.

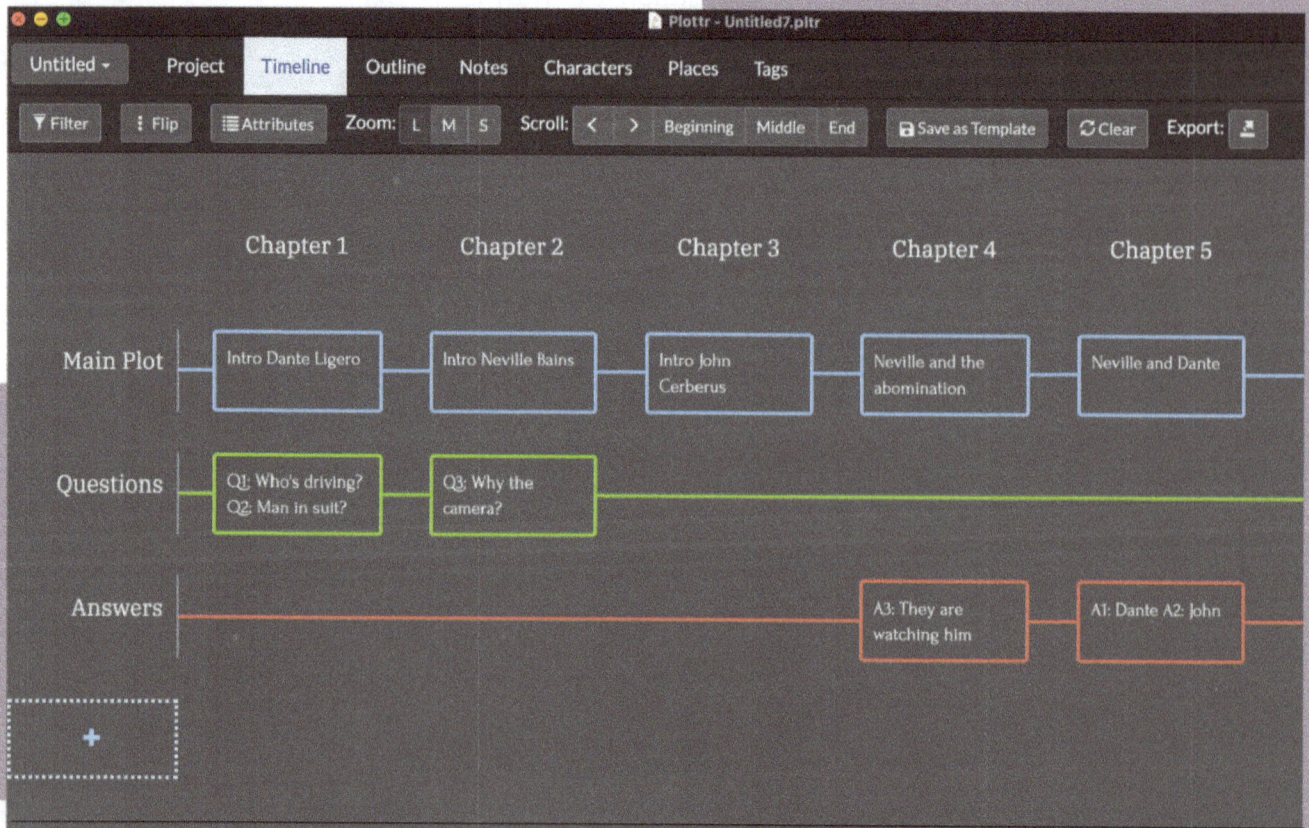

ways to organize and add vivid details to your books," Lambert recommends.

Plottr includes links to personality-trait resources, such as Enneagram and Myers-Briggs. You can leverage these in your character building, assigning custom attributes to create more rounded characters. Using the filter options, you can change the view to focus on one character, to easily track their progress through the story.

Plottr goes beyond a single book, and can help you plot and track larger story arcs. "I can easily see the timeline any way I wish. It expands as the series grows," Anderle says. If you're writing a series, Plottr's series view will let you create an outline that includes each of your titles, so you can track open loops and story threads across books.

When you are ready to explore advanced features, there are presentation options that can help you visualize the progress of your story. Individual scenes can be color-coded or tagged, according to your preferred structure. Lambert suggests using green for scenes that are completed, yellow for scenes still in progress, and red for scenes which now need to be cut.

It has the functionality that I want, while allowing me to add more details should I desire.
Michael Anderle

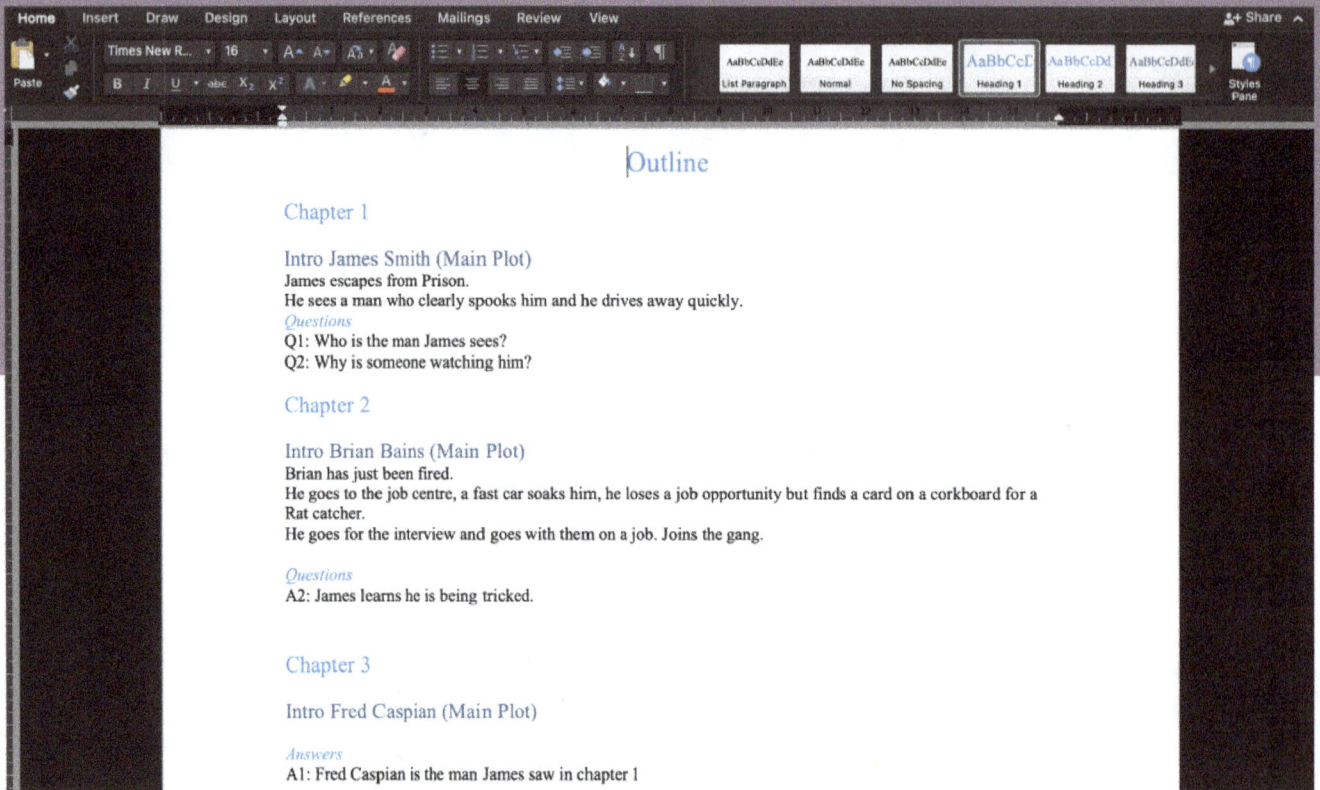

A Plottr file exported to Word, showing the Questions & Answers method for each scene.

COMPATIBILITY - HOW DOES IT LINK WITH OTHER TOOLS?

Once you've plotted your masterpiece, you need to start writing it. Plottr exports to Microsoft Word and Scrivener, two of the most popular word processors. As well as setting you up to write, this also allows you to share your plotting notes. Anderle notes "the export to Word is super useful for those who I interact with who do not use the program."

Plottr's advanced export feature lets you choose what to export to your word processor — you can now export just your scenes *or* characters *or* places *or* notes, depending on what you need. You can also specify where notes and other details will appear in your preferred word processor. Open the exported file in either program and find everything waiting for you.

Voila! No more blank screens.

There are a ton of pro authors and experienced Plottrs who will kindly step in with answers."

HELP AND SUPPORT

Plottr has many useful resources including demo videos and a free course with 46 lessons on its website (https://writelink.to/sjxvkp), and a great community on Facebook (https://www.facebook.com/groups/plottr).

Anderle praises the support available. "The programmers responded quickly when I had questions (which isn't often anymore)."

"Don't be shy about asking questions!" Lambert encourages. "There are a ton of pro authors and experienced Plottrs [in the Facebook group] who will kindly step in with answers."

Plottr also has a YouTube channel (https://writelink.to/9ijggq) with published authors. It contains outlining advice, plotting deep dives, and user-created templates you can download to help guide your thinking, as well as interviews with published authors about their processes.

AVAILABILITY

Plottr is available for PC, Mac iOS, and Android. It can be purchased as an annual subscription or a one-time lifetime purchase. At the current time, the price for a single license is $25 annually or $99 lifetime.

Available for download from www.plottr.com. ■

Elaine Bateman

Tech Tools

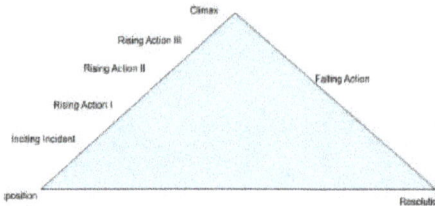	**OUTLINING A NOVEL WITH THE PLOT PYRAMID**	The plot pyramid is the first of a myriad of structures used to outline a story. Merri Maywether shows how this simple tool can lay the foundations for a well-connected story. https://writelink.to/pyzfld
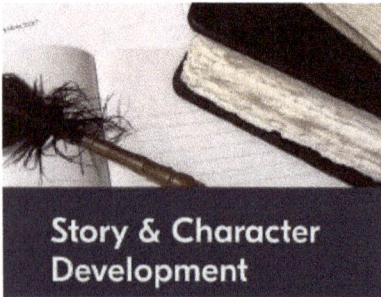	**STORY AND CHARACTER DEVELOPMENT DATABASE**	An Airtable-based database of characters, scenes, and events to help you plan your novel, sort your screenplay, and organize your fictional world so you can get writing. https://writelink.to/mzbccz
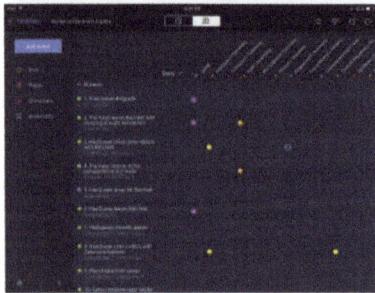	**AEON TIMELINE**	Whether you are in the opening stages of planning a novel, in the final stages of editing, or anywhere in between, Aeon Timeline has tools and features to help you track your timeline, understand your characters, avoid plot holes and inconsistencies, and visualise your story in new ways. https://writelink.to/cbplj7
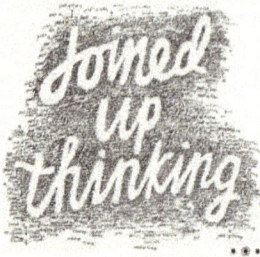	**SCRAPPLE**	A mind-mapping tool that helps you build your outline. Compatible with Scrivener, so you can export your Scapple directly to Scrivener. https://writelink.to/nxc7mo
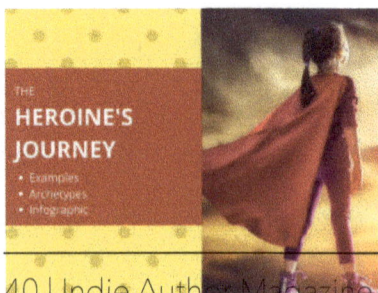	**HEROINE'S JOURNEY**	The StoryGrid team looks at what sets the heroine's journey apart from its more famous male counterpart, the hero's journey. https://writelink.to/gz8uk0

A Matter of Trust

MAKING YOUR COVER MATCH YOUR GENRE

Imagine you're on Amazon, scrolling through hundreds of books when you come across this cover.

What do you think? It's arguably different from the other covers on the page.

How do you feel about it? What about the story? Is it your thing or perhaps something that you text a friend because it reminds you of them?

I commissioned this cover for a solid action-adventure, but over and over again, when faced with those questions, my readers answered the same way:

"I don't know."

It wasn't bad art—many readers complemented the Saul Bass style. Those that read the few books I had before had an inkling of my genre, but didn't give this a second look. Some took a chance after passing it by several times like the mayo and white bread sandwich it looked like.

They just didn't know what THIS story was about (other than perhaps a sword and a motorcycle).

Don't hear what I am not saying—I LOVE this cover and the artist gave me EXACTLY what I asked for. But for its purpose—to draw people into the world beyond this image—it fails.

It lays there, doing and saying nothing, offering no promise of what you will find beyond it.

If you didn't figure out that this is an urban fantasy with a hardass female lead, then this is the reason why we're writing this

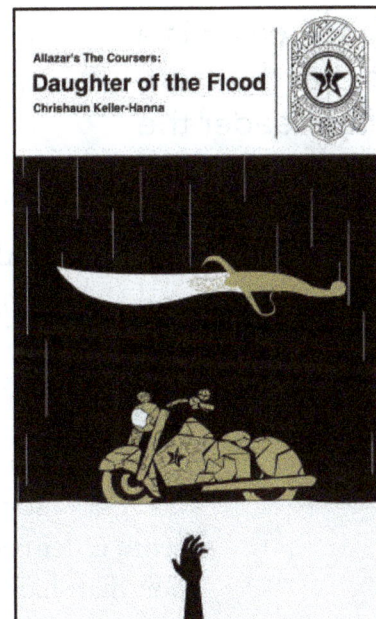

article. Thousands of writers see their cover as an expression of their artistic sensibilities or a direct translation of the story within.

And while it can be that, those are secondary considerations.

A book cover is a promise that the story will give the reader the escape, emotion, and excitement that the cover portrays. The goal of the cover above all other things is to instill trust.

A trust that's developed by filling the cover with elements that proclaim "YES, THIS IS THE BOOK YOU WANT!" or at least "This has everything you want in a story."

To gain that sort of trust, we have to rethink what we know about genre.

When you hear the word "genre," you think "sci-fi," "high fantasy," "romance," etc. This makes sense—genre is defined as a category of artistic composition that shares a type of form, style, or subject matter.

Each category has elements that all the stories share to some degree. No matter the author, there's always a love story in a romance, and there's magic of some shape or form in high fantasy.

By extension, book covers that tell the same type of story have similar images, composition, colors, and fonts. It creates a world that you can quickly identify with and draws you in.

> A book cover is a promise that the story will give the reader the escape, emotion, and excitement that the cover portrays. The goal of the cover above all other things is to instill trust.

> Book covers that tell the same type of story have similar images, composition, colors, and fonts.

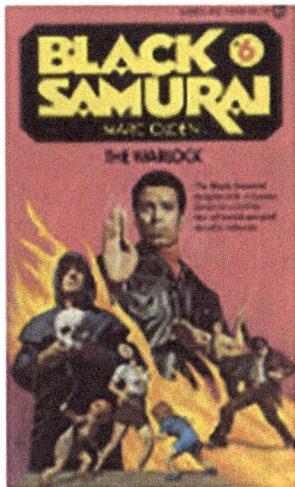

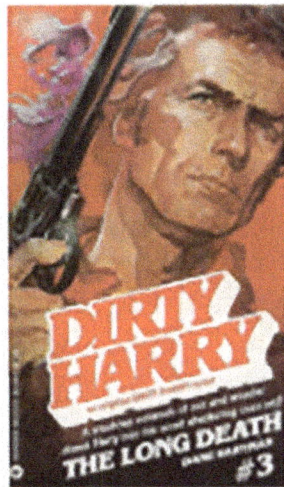

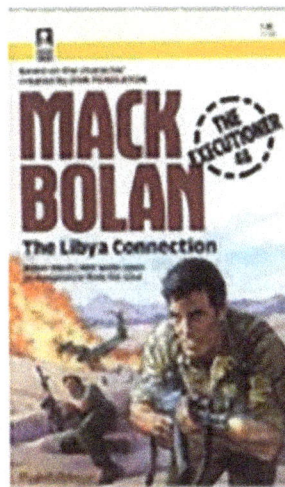

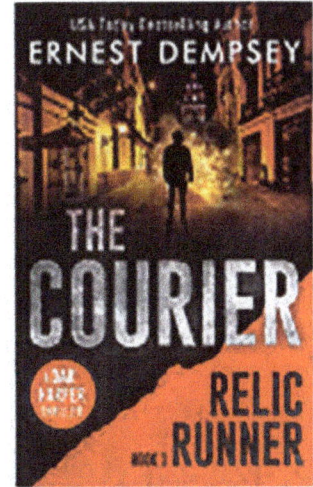

Let's take an example from one of my favorite genres.

These covers range from 1976 to 2021. They all share a dominant, bold font, the character's name is much bigger than the title of the book.

The protagonist is the focus, surrounded by red, red fire, and firepower and various things that mean to kill him.

These covers are not only very explicit about their genre but are trying to elicit strong emotions from you. Strong enough that you will stop, click on that cover, and buy it.

When you look at other covers in your genre, what are the common images, colors, framing elements, and fonts you see?

For Daughter of the Flood, I had to pull from several places. Since Duke, my main character, is a bounty hunter, I looked at action and bounty hunter books.

I noticed the action novels that caught my eye have strong, warm colors, with the protagonist featured in front and the titles were short and to the point.

Duke chases specters that escape the Ether, so I looked at hundreds of urban fantasy and paranormal romance covers. Here I found that the colors were cooler (more blues and purples), with the protagonist (usually a woman with glowing hands and/or eyes) front and center.

But what caught my eye is how urban fantasy covers use the background as worldbuilding. Whether it's the gates of a school, the mean streets (which are always wet for some reason), or the forest where humans turn to animals, with a glance you know if you've arrived or taken a wrong turn.

Give some thought to what single feeling you want to rush over the reader. And use every element and trope to reinforce that.

The new author always wants their story to stand out from the thousands of other offerings out there. And of course—the book that is seen is the one that's clicked on.

But being too original, like the Daughter of the Flood cover referenced earlier, risks losing an opportunity to stir up emotions and connect. The same elements are used because they're proven effective in doing just that.

However, there's some wiggle room, if you just can't bear the thought of putting yet another girl with glowing hands on a wet back alley on your urban fantasy novel.

Look at covers in your genre from different decades or international editions for fresh ideas that still work.

In the revamped cover, I used the Arizona desert with the colors bumped up to let you know that this might be on Earth, but there's something alien about it as well.

The bold and gritty font promises action and adventure, and the disheveled woman on a Harley looking into the distance tells you there'll be some blood and profanity in your future. I also changed the title to one of Duke's best lines—it's the entire plot in five words.

The difference between the two covers is striking. And the new cover is more effective because the focus is on what the readers expect rather than my need for artistic expression.

That's hard to let go of, but what you get in return are readers that will follow you anywhere. ▪

Chrishaun Keller-Hanna

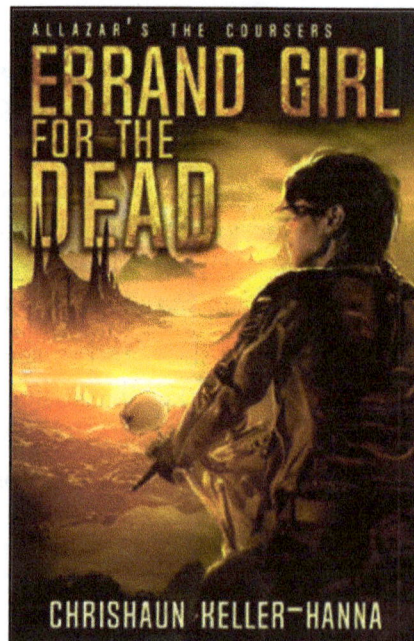

DEVIL IN THE DETAILS:

FIGHT SCENES

You've decided that violence is the answer! In your story, that is, but now what? What makes a good fight? There are a lot of things to consider for your scene to come across as authentic and credible to your audience. There's a reason choreographers map out fights to be filmed; **to fight is to dance**. As the writer you get to decide what kind of dance your characters are doing.

With hand to hand combat, the size and body types of your combatants matters. Large fighters are generally slower but only need a few good hits. Smaller characters need to be faster, more accurate, and to use momentum against their opponents. Biologically male characters have more strength in their upper bodies; biologically female characters' strength is in their core and quads. Weapons have weight or kickback; this can wear a fighter down depending on their physicality.

Don't forget sensory cues — getting hit hurts!

Depending on where you're hit, it can be debilitating. Head shots versus body shots can make a huge difference. Hitting soft tissue, or hard muscle, or solid bone feels and hurts differently. Sounds can become distorted if you have blood in your ears. These details all work together to enhance the reader's immersion into your world.

Setting is key to your details. It tells you what is available to your characters for a fight in the physical world around them. Visualize and inventory what they have at hand in a spontaneous fight. The type of terrain or building structure can add to the tension of your fight. High land is advantaged with a weapon, but coming from low land can make it easier to knock an opponent off balance.

Natural ability only gets a fighter so far. A character can bolster some of the physical attributes with training. Endurance can be trained. Strength and flexibility can be nominally increased. Strategy can be learned. To maintain plausibility, you need to know the tenets and principles of the training the character has received. Whether it is martial arts or yoga, or from a policing/military organization or a magical academy, the details of the general progression and the associated value system matter.

> Endurance can be trained. Strength and flexibility can be nominally increased. Strategy can be learned.

If your character is a former military, you need to know not only what they're capable of, but how they're going to react to a threat in hand-to-hand combat. If they react in a way that is incompatible with their training, it could jar the reader and break their suspension of disbelief.

The same goes for martial arts: the belt progression takes time. Even when you're naturally talented, you have to complete the required hours to progress to the next level. Each form of martial arts has different specialties.

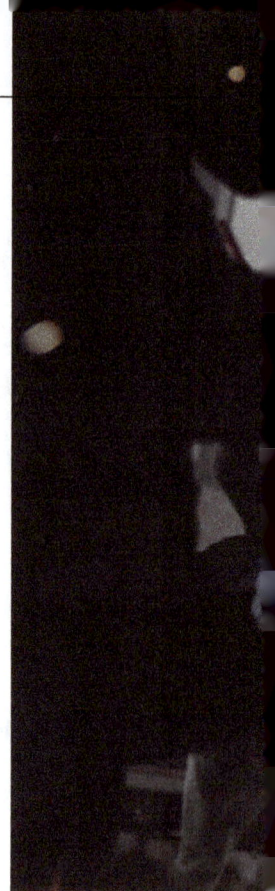

Understanding what is naturally possible is critical to keeping your fight dynamics believable

For example, traditional Tae Kwon Do is a martial art with a lot of kicks. Kicks aren't always practical in a fight. Legs are easy to grab and twist. Well-executed kicks require speed and accuracy. You also need to know how to break holds so you don't get your leg torn off.

Traditional Tae Kwon Do focuses on training formations or forms, as preparation for being attacked by multiple opponents. Olympic-style Tae Kwon Do (the more popular iteration today) is sparring based, and therefore focuses on one-on-one fighting. Using a technique in the wrong circumstance breaks the character's credibility as an expert fighter.

Chemically altering bodies, cyborg prosthetics, and magic all change your character's strength and movement, but understanding what is naturally possible versus what would need those enhancements is critical to keeping your fight dynamics believable. ■

Sìne Màiri MacDougall

De-Mystery-fying Tropes

A mystery is a crime or puzzle that must be solved by the end of the story. It is critical to reader expectation and satisfaction that the culprit is discovered, and justice is seen to be done. The driving force is the main character's quest to solve the mystery, creating intrigue until the climatic end when the antagonist's identity is revealed. This is achieved through the protagonist's intelligence, logical interpretation of clues, and sometimes luck, although red herrings are used to purposefully mislead and prevent readers from predicting the outcome. Most importantly, the author must play fair, so readers have every chance to solve the crime before the sleuth.

Mystery subgenres are often confused with mystery tropes from their strong illustration, but they are not themselves tropes. Amazon and Barnes and Noble list categories of mystery sub-genres, such as amateur sleuth, private eye, and police procedural, etc, and even go deeper into sub-sub-genres like cozy-hobbies and crafts.

Tropes are plot devices or themes within genres that readers have come to expect, where some are non-negotiable, while others can be

> Tropes are plot devices or themes within genres that readers have come to expect

used in a variety of ways. Mystery has a standard use of tropes, such as "the eccentric detective" or even "a locked room mystery," and a possible list can be found on the website, TvTropes. Choosing them wisely can enable marketing, piquing reader attention and drumming up interest.

While tropes are unavoidable, they aren't necessarily the same as cliches. "Ten Little Murder Victims" is a popular trope where an isolated group of people must find the killer amongst them

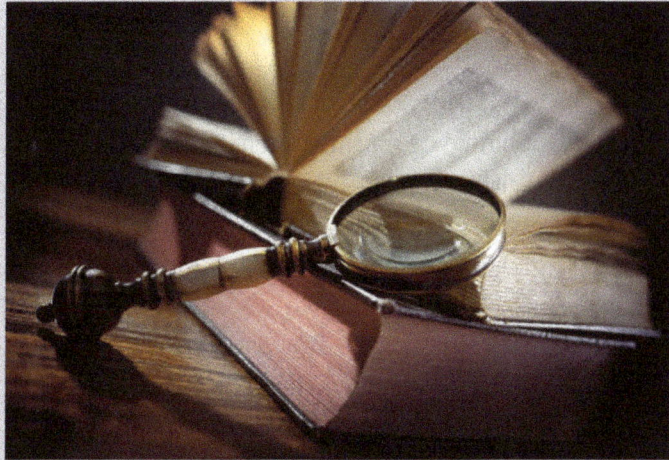

TEN MYSTERY TROPES

before most of them die. In contrast, the clichéd "the police don't know how to do their job" can be an overused and tired trope that lacks original thought if the author doesn't add anything new. Even though tropes are entertaining, and readers have their favorites, there are also ones they dislike, especially when harmful—e.g., groups of people are negatively stereotyped.

1. The eccentric detective: the trope was popularized with the characters Sherlock Holmes and Hercule Poirot.
2. The protagonist is a suspect: creates the protagonist's need to solve the crime and allows readers to experience the investigation from the main character's point of view.
3. Hateful victim: any number of suspects who may have had an axe to grind to cause the victim's death.
4. The snitch as cannon fodder: a safe-to-kill side character not integral to the main character team.
5. Isolated house party: where the cast are kept isolated and one of them is the killer.
6. Mistaken identity: a character is killed when they were thought to be someone else.
7. Never the obvious suspect: suspect has obvious motive and opportunity, but someone else is the culprit.
8. You meddling kids: the antagonist would've succeeded with their crime if it weren't for the protagonist.
9. You wake up in a room: a character wakes up in an unfamiliar location.
10. Mystery magnet: the protagonist seems to attract mysteries.

Choosing likeable tropes allows a greater chance of making them engaging, while writing with intention often crafts tropes in an original way. This elevates the story while avoiding it becoming cliché and unintentionally detracting.

Subverting a cliché can freshen it so the reader does not get the expected result, such as "the butler did it," where the butler is set up and the antagonist takes that opportunity to try to get away. An example of a cliché repurposed for a new audience is using a character type who doesn't normally get to solve the crime, like a disabled protagonist.

The film Knives Out used tropes associated with the mystery genre, including "a murder occurs on a large estate," "they know more than they let on," and "the heart of a person outweighs their deeds." The "mysterious benefactor" trope was subverted when the killer hired the detective to frame the protagonist, and "the detective did suspect the protagonist but was going to let her off and rule as suicide" because of "the heart of the person outweighs their deeds" trope. (George Chrysostomou, https://screenrant.com/knives-out-rian-johnson-crime-tropes)

Another subversion of a mystery trope is possibly the clueless mystery. Overall, readers like to play along with the protagonist, but in a clueless mystery, the audience is expected to sit back and follow the main character as they get to the bottom of things. This situation may have come about after readers complained the clues are too easy but can leave them feeling cheated due to being unable to beat the detective. Clearly then, tropes are a double-edged sword that must be wielded with both knowledge and caution. ∎

Anne Lown

> **Tropes are a double-edged sword that must be wielded with both knowledge and caution.**

For more information on this topic, check out:

Craig Martelle's Successful Indie Author Five-Minute Focus on Tropes vs Cliches
https://writelink.to/nnohp4

Jenna Moreci's video on Tropes vs Cliches
https://writelink.to/4dkgvj

Play
to
Win

Stack
the Odds
in Your Favor
with the Friday Five
from Indie Author Tools.
A free weekly email with the
best indie author tips, tools, and tech.

https://writelink.to/iat

Small Starts, Big Gains: Move Your Body

As writers, there is nothing better than finding ourselves in the creative zone of genius, furiously pumping out words for hours at a time. Before you realize it, you've gone a whole day sitting in one spot, realizing only when you stand up that your joints should not sound like popping bubble wrap.

It's possible that the very thing we love—getting lost in the words for hours at a time—could be contributing to our declining health. Recent studies published in the International Journal of Behavioral Nutrition and Physical Activity (IJBNPA) suggest that even very moderate exercise can help decrease the risk of heart attack, stroke, type 2 diabetes, and some cancers.

Chances are you've ticked more than one of the risk factor boxes. Most of us do. So how do we beat back our slothful tendencies while also staying in the creative flow? Here are some tips.

TIMED STANDING BREAKS EVERY HOUR.

Set an alarm on your watch or computer to remind you to stand up, even for a few minutes, and be sure you do it. Most smartwatches have this functionality built-in with no need for an extra app. Don't make this a huge endeavor. Simply stretch, touch your toes and get the blood flowing for 2-3 minutes.

STAY HYDRATED

Without proper hydration, your body won't want to move. Keep a water bottle near you at all times. Apps like Waterminder are great for tracking your intake as well as reminding you when you should drink more. (writelink.to/water)

CONSIDER A STANDING DESK OR DICTATE WHILE WALKING

There are documented benefits for using a standing desk. (writelink.to/ttbsd) While standing doesn't burn significantly more calories than sitting, it does provide some benefit in reducing pain and inflammation, and studies show that blood sugar levels regulate more quickly. Walking, however, is an excellent low-impact method of exercise, and some authors prefer to multitask—dictating their first drafts while also taking a stroll around the block.

Start small. Make and keep little promises to yourself to move more. The inertia of getting up several times a day will train your body and your brain to crave more movement, and you'll find that it becomes easier over time. And who knows? The words you create while caring for your body could become a big gain to your readership and bank account too. ■

Chelle Honiker

DEFINING SUCCESS

Many of us write because we love to write; it's our outlet that keeps us sane. Publishing is a by-product that becomes our businesses to pay for our writing habits. This means we need to make decisions, sometimes difficult ones, on how we proceed with our business. No one wants to burn out.

In order to figure out our pace, first we need to define what success means for us. This is personal—breaking even, becoming solvent by paying off debt, or going full time. It's going to look different for every individual. You need a strategy that works for you. There are plenty of books available on strategy, but even before you look at them you need to sit down and ask yourself:

- **What do I want?**
- **What are my goals to get what I want?**
- **What is feasible?**
- **What am I willing to do in the short term to reach my goal?**

Many writers use the fiscal year to plan out the year. While this can be useful, setting yourself up to work in your own natural cycles within that is extremely beneficial. From there, breaking down goals into trackable metrics can help you gauge your growth. Newsletter open rates and social media can be great ways to measure progression. Celebrate the little successes that lead to bigger success.

Whether you want to keep your day job or become a full time author is entirely up to you. Writing part-time doesn't make you any less successful than someone who is full time. Find your own definition of success, put it front and center each day. And strive to hit that mark every single day. ■

Sìne Màiri MacDougall

> Find your own definition of success, put it front and center each day. And strive to hit that mark every single day.

WIDE VS. EXCLUSIVE: WHICH IS FOR YOU?

GLOSSARY

Aggregator a company which distributes e-books to multiple retail platforms.

Distributor a company which makes e-books available to readers via retail platforms.

Exclusive exclusive to Amazon's KDP Select program, also called KU.

KDP Select the author facing side for the Kindle Unlimited program. KDP Select requires e-books to be offered exclusive to them, and available no where else.

KU Kindle Unlimited, the reader facing side of KDP Select.

Wide not exclusive to Amazon's KDP Select program, also called KU. Many authors make their e-books available on as many platforms as possible when wide.

"Should you go wide?" is one of the most popular questions in Indie publishing. "Wide" publishing means offering your e-book(s) in as many channels, languages, countries, and formats as you can. The alternative to wide is referred to as "exclusive," which is signing with Amazon's KDP Select program, often just called "KU" (referring to Kindle Unlimited - the reader side of KDP Select.)

You have already made hundreds of decisions about your book(s) — main characters, points of view, length, genre, tropes, etc. — the craft decisions. The publishing decisions are no different as an indie author. You decide everything too.

> Print and audio books can always be wide, even if e-books are in KDP Select.

FIVE QUESTIONS TO ASK YOURSELF IF GOING WIDE IS FOR YOU:

1. DO YOU WANT TO DIVE OR WADE INTO THE PUBLISHING POOL?

You may be the kind of author who doesn't want to sign any exclusivity agreements, or you may decide being exclusive with Amazon is a way to start small and learn as you go. Before you spend the time setting up an account with every retailer you might publish in KU and, after the time required to stay in the program has expired, then go wide.

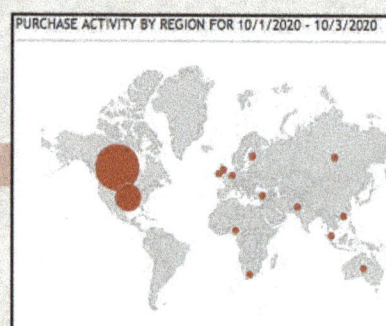

Kobo Writing Life Map showing the growth of the author's reach after 3 titles published.

2. WHERE ARE YOU IN YOUR PUBLISHING CAREER?

With only one (or two) books published, you can be invisible. Don't immediately decide your book is bad or your marketing is wrong. Some authors don't see traction until the third title is published. (See Kobo Writing Life map for this author's example.) Readers, retailers, and algorithms all prefer a solid history with a platform. Sometimes, a "failed" strategy may work wonderfully at a later stage in your career.

3. DO YOU WANT TO DIVERSIFY YOUR INCOME OR HAVE ALL YOUR EGGS IN ONE BASKET?

Authors need to weigh the pros and cons between the time investment of setting up and tracking every platform versus weathering the risks inherent in dips in KU payment fluctuations. These fluctuations are factors beyond the author's control, since they share a pool of income with every other author in KU.

4. DO YOU LIKE TO PLAY IT SAFE? OR DO YOU PREFER TO EXPLORE UNCHARTED REGIONS?

Many authors get into publishing wide because of all the countries they can reach. Through wide distributors and aggregators, you have access to many more marketplaces worldwide

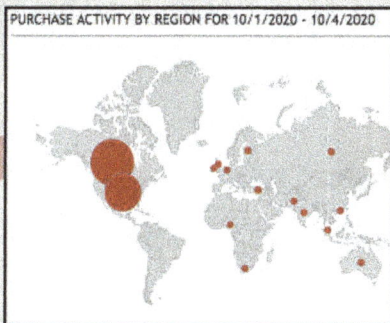

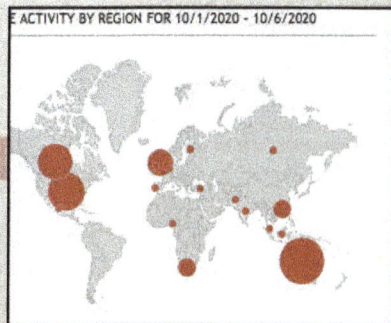

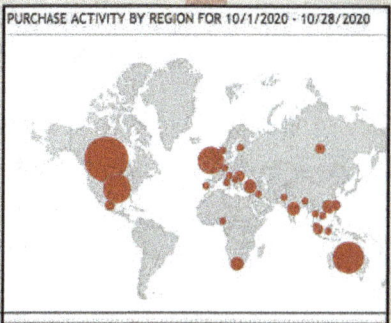

than you do with Amazon alone. If truly worldwide accessibility is important to you, wide may be your best option. One of the most delightful things about being wide is watching your Kobo Writing Life map explode when you do your first successful promotion.

5. DOES DATA EXCITE YOU?

The amount of work involved conducting experiments and tracking information from every account can be daunting if you're not an organized and analytical person. If you are a "you never know unless you try" sort of author, you might like being wide. You can speed up your progress by keeping track of what works for your books and what doesn't. Then do more of what works.

Wide authors have more administrative details to keep track of. At the bare minimum, it would be helpful to keep a spreadsheet of where your books are distributed and with which aggregators. This will help you catch mistakes, like listing a book twice on the same store.

IF YOU DECIDE TO PUBLISH EXCLUSIVELY TO AMAZON

Tick the "enroll in KDP Select" box when you upload your book to Amazon. Your publishing deliberations are over.

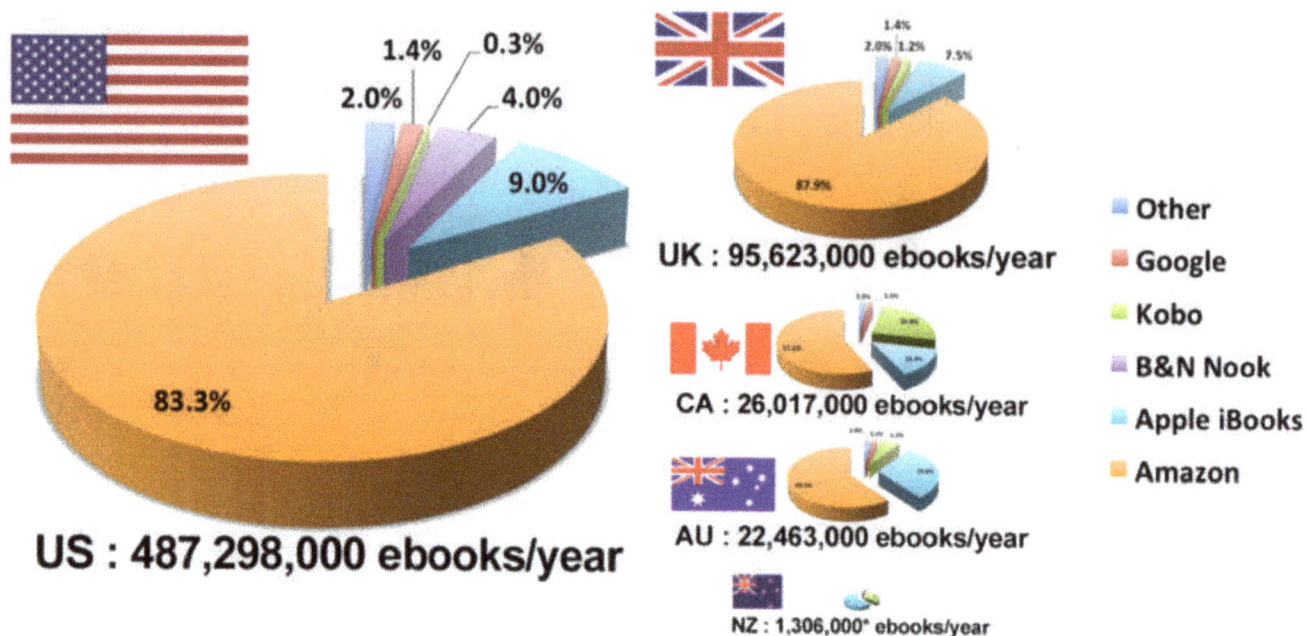

US : 487,298,000 ebooks/year

83.3%
9.0%
4.0%
2.0%
1.4%
0.3%

UK : 95,623,000 ebooks/year

CA : 26,017,000 ebooks/year

AU : 22,463,000 ebooks/year

NZ : 1,306,000* ebooks/year

Other
Google
Kobo
B&N Nook
Apple iBooks
Amazon

(Source of image: authorearnings.com)
Found on Publish Drive: writelink.to/mktshr

IF YOU DECIDE TO PUBLISH WIDE

You immediately have two more decisions:

1. Which retailers should you list on, and
2. Should you upload your books directly to the retailer or use an aggregator?

An aggregator is a service that forwards your book information to retailers. Amazon and Apple are retailers. Aggregators include Draft-2Digital, Streetlib, Smashwords, and Publish-Drive. (Just to confuse things, Kobo and Tolino are both retailers and aggregators.)

Mark Leslie Lefebvre's *Wide for the Win* takes a helpful detailed look at many distributors and retailers. Or study the details on each retailer's site for yourself.

CAN I CHANGE MY MIND?

Short answer: Yes, you can. It is often recommended for new authors to start in KU for simplicity, and then move wide as they gain experience and navigate the intricacies of the indie publishing world. The downside to this is that you will then need to rebuild your audience wide, as there is not a lot of overlap between the two groups of readers. It may depend on your genre and other factors as well. If you are overwhelmed with all the choices and moving pieces of the publishing journey, this is a valid choice to make whether or not you choose to go wide later. This is the great part of being Indie - you have the freedom and flexibility to change your mind!

Laurel Decher

WIDE RESOURCES

- *Wide for the Win* by Mark Leslie Lefebvre, Stark Publishing Solutions, 2021, 406 pgs.
- *How to Market a Book: Overperform in a Crowded Market* by Ricardo Fayet. Section V covers "Wide Marketing." Reedsy, 2021. https://reedsy.com/discovery/book/how-to-market-a-book-overperform-in-a-crowded-market-ricardo-fayet
- *Going Wide Unboxed: The Three-Year No-Bestseller Plan for Making a Living From Your Fiction* by Patty Jansen. Capricornica Publications, 2017.
- "The ONE RIGHT WAY TO SELL BOOKS" How to Self-Publish with the SPA Girls podcast (Trudi Jaye, Cheryl Phipps, Wendy Vella and Shar Barratt), episode 273, Jan 5, 2021. https://coronitas.link/phtdjw
- "Top 10 Tips to Going Wide" by Erin Wright, June 26, 2020 https://writelink.to/qub1cp
- Wide for the Win Facebook group. Admins: Erin Wright and Suzie O'Connell. https://writelink.to/ebmf58
- The International Indie Author Facebook group. Admin: Mark Williams. https://writelink.to/ebmf58
- *The New Publishing Standard* edited by Mark Williams. https://writelink.to/wiuz0l

Books We Love

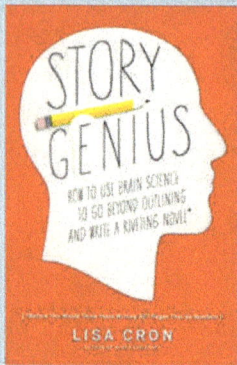

Following on the heels of Lisa Cron's breakout first book, *Wired for Story,* this writing guide reveals how to use cognitive storytelling strategies to build a scene-by-scene blueprint for a riveting story.

It's every novelist's greatest fear: pouring their blood, sweat, and tears into writing hundreds of pages only to realize that their story has no sense of urgency, no internal logic, and so is a page one rewrite.

The prevailing wisdom in the writing community is that there are just two ways around this problem: pantsing (winging it) and plotting (focusing on the external plot). Story coach Lisa Cron has spent her career discovering why these methods don't work and coming up with a powerful alternative, based on the science behind what our brains are wired to crave in every story we read (and it's not what you think).

In *Story Genius* Cron takes you, step-by-step, through the creation of a novel from the first glimmer of an idea, to a complete multilayered blueprint—including fully realized scenes—that evolves into a first draft with the authority, richness, and command of a riveting sixth or seventh draft.

https://indieauthortools.com/story-genius/

Writing a well-structured romance isn't the same as writing any other genre—something the popular novel and screenwriting guides don't address. The romance arc is made up of its own story beats, and the external plot and theme need to be braided to the romance arc—not the other way around.

Told in conversational (and often irreverent) prose, *Romancing the Beat* can be read like you are sitting down to coffee with romance editor and author Gwen Hayes while she explains story structure. The way she does with her clients. Some of whom are regular inhabitants of the New York Times and USA Today bestseller lists.

Romancing the Beat is a recipe, not a rigid system. The beats don't care if you plot or outline before you write, or if you pants your way through the drafts and do a "beat check" when you're revising. Pantsers and plotters are both welcome. So sit down, grab a cuppa, and let's talk about kissing books.

https://indieauthortools.com/romancing-the-beat-story-structure-for-romance-novels/

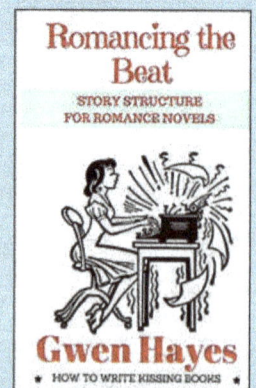

Now Pantsers Can Benefit From Simplified Plotting

Whether you are a bestseller or an aspiring author, this planning workbook will help you keep your characters, plot, and timeline straight.

With pages to detail your locations, characters, scenes, plot points, etc., this workbook organizes all the prewriting, writing, and post-production aspects of getting a book into print.

https://indieauthortools.com/pantsers-plotting-planning-workbook-25/

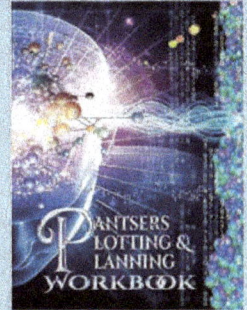

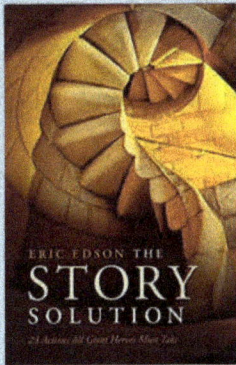

Eric Edson, a master teacher of screenwriting, shares his blueprint for writing blockbuster movies. His technique features 23 "hero goal steps," which he says are used in every successful movie to create dynamic, three-dimensional heroes all linked to plot structure and the plot points of a captivating screenplay.

https://indieauthortools.com/the-story-solution-23-steps-all-great-heroes-must-take/

John Truby is one of the most respected and sought-after story consultants in the film industry, and his students have gone on to pen some of Hollywood's most successful films, including Sleepless in Seattle, Scream, and Shrek. The Anatomy of Story is his long-awaited first book, and it shares all his secrets for writing a compelling script. Based on the lessons in his award-winning class, Great Screenwriting, The Anatomy of Story draws on a broad range of philosophy and mythology, offering fresh techniques and insightful anecdotes alongside Truby's own unique approach to building an effective, multifaceted narrative.

https://indieauthortools.com/anatomy-of-story-22-steps-to-becoming-a-master-storyteller/

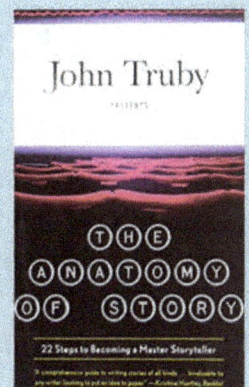

INDIE AUTHOR NEWS

SCRIVENER 3

Scrivener 3 is a major update to Scrivener now available for both macOS and Windows that not only brings some very cool new features but also improves and simplifies what was already there.

If you purchased Scrivener 2 for macOS on or after August 20, 2017, you can update to Scrivener 3 for free. If you purchased earlier, you can update with a 45% discount.

If you purchased Scrivener 1 for Windows on or after November 20, 2017, you can update to Scrivener 3 for free. If you purchased earlier, you can update with a 49% discount.

https://writelink.to/scrivener

THE COVER DESIGNER DIRECTORY

The Cover Designer Directory was recently launched. It provides a curated selection of high-quality, indie-minded, talented, and ethical cover designers.

https://writelink.to/38n2fl

STORYORIGIN OUT OF BETA

The long-running beta phase of StoryOrigin has ended, and a new pricing structure was introduced. The free plan still allows file delivery and word-count tracking, but group promos, newsletter swaps, and email collection are now paid features ($10/month or $100/year.)

https://writelink.to/jagxn7

CLUBHOUSE FOR ANDROID

Clubhouse is expected to be available to Android users in May

KDP TO BE EPUB ONLY

Amazon KDP is switching to EPUB only. After June 28, 2021, Amazon will no longer support MOBI files when publishing new or updating previously published reflowable eBooks. Instead, use EPUB, DOCX, or KPF formats for uploads. Existing titles do not need to be changed unless you re-upload the document.

https://writelink.to/r6ir8x

Got news or events to share with
the Indie Author Community?
Let us know at
news@indieauthormagazine.com.

HOOTSUITE CHANGES

Hootsuite's Free plan has changed. Hootsuite is a social media management tool. You can now only manage 2 social accounts and schedule up to 5 posts with the Free plan; other functionality is now paid, starting from $49/month.
https://writelink.to/efalyh

VELLA

On April 13, 2021, Amazon announced the launch of Kindle Vella. U.S. based authors can publish serialized stories, one short episode at a time. Here's what we know so far:

- Episodes must be in English and between 600-5,000 words.
- You can't break down a previously published book (or other long-form content) into Episodes and republish in Kindle Vella, even if that book is no longer available or is written in another language.
- You can't convert a Vella story to a book without first removing all episodes from the Vella platform.
- If you have a serialized story available elsewhere, you can also publish it with Kindle Vella.
- You'll earn 50% of what readers spend on the Tokens that are used to unlock your story's episodes.
- The first few episodes of every story are free.
- The number of Tokens needed to unlock an episode is determined by the episode's word count at the rate of one token per 100 words.
- Cost of Tokens (and thus royalties to authors) are still unclear.
- Only open to US based authors at present, though the speculation is that this will be rolled out to other territories once the beta phase is complete.
https://writelink.to/u06ggg

IAM OPINIONATED

Kindle Vella - Future of Publishing or Just a Fad?
Have your say!
Vote here
https://writelink.to/iamopinionated

INDIE AUTHOR EVENTS

June

June 4-6, 2021

The Author Conference on Clubhouse

https://writelink.to/2mzes4

June 4-6, 2021

SFWA Nebula Awards

https://writelink.to/addox7

June 11-13, 2021

SFFCon - The Science Fiction & Fantasy Convention virtual conference

https://www.facebook.com/groups/sffcon/

July

July 17 - August 1, 2021

InkersCon 2021 Digital Conference

3 weekends of online networking and events.
https://writelink.to/qaxeji

Got news or events to share with
the Indie Author Community?
Let us know at
news@indieauthormagazine.com.

November

November 8-12

20Books Vegas

The largest conference for indie authors, all about the business of self-publishing.
Indie Author Magazine will be there—will you? (You must be a member of the free 20Books to 50K® group to attend the conference.)
https://writelink.to/20Books

December

December 15-19

DisCon III

The 79th World Science Fiction Convention (aka Worldcon) has changed its dates. Usually Worldcon is held in August, but this year it is December 15-19. The host city is still Washington DC, and the program will combine in-person and virtual events. A Virtual Membership, to access the online programming, will start at US$75.
https://writelink.to/owbxyk

In This Issue

Executive Team

Chelle Honiker, Publisher

As the publisher of Indie Author Magazine, Chelle Honiker brings nearly three decades of startup, technology, training, and executive leadership experience to the role. She's a serial entrepreneur, founding and selling multiple successful companies including a training development company, travel agency, website design and hosting firm, a digital marketing consultancy, and a wedding planning firm. She's organized and curated multiple TEDx events and hired to assist other nonprofit organizations as a fractional executive, including The Travel Institute and The Freelance Association.

As a writer, speaker, and trainer she believes in the power of words and their ability to heal, inspire, incite, and motivate. Her greatest inspiration is her daughters, Kelsea and Cathryn, who tolerate her tendency to run away from home to play with her friends around the world for months at a time. It's said she could run a small country with just the contents of her backpack.

Alice Briggs, Creative Director

As the creative director of Indie Author Magazine, Alice Briggs utilizes her more than three decades of artistic exploration and expression, business startup adventures, and leadership skills. A serial entrepreneur, she has started several successful businesses. She brings her experience in creative direction, magazine layout and design, and graphic design in and outside of the indie author community to her role.

With a masters of science in Occupational Therapy, she has a broad skill set and uses it to assist others in achieving their desired goals. As a writer, teacher, healer, and artist, she loves to see people accomplish all they desire. She's excited to see how IAM will encourage many authors to succeed in whatever way they choose. She hopes to meet many of you in various places around the world once her passport is back in use.

Erika Everest, Managing Editor

Over fifteen years in the corporate sector, managing international projects and teams, gives Erika Everest a strong foundation for managing the globally-dispersed editorial team working at Indie Author Magazine.

She has co-curated eight anthologies in the past three years, and works with authors for proofreading, beta reading, editing, formatting, and newsletter set up and maintenance.

With a PhD in Biostatistics and a postgraduate qualification in International Business Management, Erika values strategic and analytical thinking. She also values unicorns, tiaras, and happily ever afters. She has published three novels in a series of fairytale retellings, and likes to procrastinate by writing nonfiction books to help authors.

Robyn Sarty, Managing Editor

As a managing editor at Indie Author Magazine, Robyn Sarty brings over a decade of experience as an editor and proofreader. She is the author of two novels and several short stories, and manages her own publishing company. She loves helping other authors with their books and can often be found nerding out over story elements with her friends. She spent five years as a project coordinator for an international engineering firm, and now uses those skills to chase writers instead of engineers and hopes it will be good training for her first marathon.

Growing up as a third culture kid, books were the one constant in her life, and as such, Robyn believes that books are portals to the magic that lies within, and authors are wielders of that magic. She also admits to being a staunch, loyal, and unabashed supporter of the Oxford comma.

Staff Writers

Elaine Bateman

In her pre-author life, Elaine worked for FTSE 100 and Fortune 500 companies in procurement, project support, and IT Training. She has a bachelor of scienceBSc. in Systems Practice and Design.

She is the author of eight published fiction novels and is working on her ninth.

Elaine enjoys giving back to the writing community through her work with 20Booksto50k, an online author community.

She was the Acorn Sports Bar Ladies' Yard-of-Ale Speed-drinking champion of 1985 (she was the only lady to enter and it took her all night.)

She lives in the UK with her husband, son, and three dogs. She no longer drinks ale.

Laurel Decher

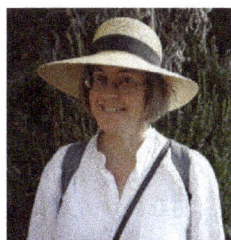

There might be no frigate like a book, but publishing can feel like a voyage on the H.M.S. Surprise. There's always a twist and there's never a moment to lose.

Laurel's mission is to help you make the most of today's opportunities. She's a strategic problem-solver, tool collector, and co-inventor of the "you never know" theory of publishing.

As an epidemiologist, she studied factors that help babies and toddlers thrive. Now she writes books for children ages nine to twelve about finding more magic in life. She's a member of the Society for Children's Book Writers and Illustrators (SCBWI), has various advanced degrees, and a tendency to smuggle vegetables into storylines.

Marion Hermannsen

Marion is a bilingual author, working in both German and English. She holds a masters of artsan MA in English, Spanish, and Italian, as well as a DipM (Marketing). She spent thirteen years both in London and Ireland while working in the finance and consulting industry.

Marion loves learning about writing craft and marketing best practices. She spends time mentoring other writers and enjoys the freedom of being able to work from anywhere.

She now lives in Frankfurt and is an active member of the local writing community, having published eight novels to date.

Her Irish husband has not only taught her the benefits of drinking copious amounts of black tea, but has impressed his Irish accent on her, to the amusement of her friends and colleagues.

Chrishaun Keller-Hanna

Chrishaun Keller-Hanna is an award-winning journalist, teacher, technical writer, and fiction author that lives for explaining difficult concepts in a way that non-technical readers can understand.

She spent twenty years teaching literacy and composition to a variety of students from kindergarten to college level and writing technical documentation for several tech companies in the Austin area. At the age of forty-three, she decided to write fiction and has published over thirty titles so far with plans to extend out to comics and board games.

When she's not writing, she's traveling, playing video games, or watching movies. When she's not doing THAT, she's talking about them with her husband and grown daughters.

Kasia Lasinska

Kasia Lasinska holds an LLB in Law with European Legal Studies and an LL.M. in Advanced Studies in International Law. As a practicing attorney, Kasia worked with a top international human rights barrister and then advised clients at a large, international law firm. These inspired her to write dystopian and fantasy novels about corrupt governments and teenagers saving the world.

Kasia lived in eight countries and speaks five languages (fluently after a glass of wine). She currently lives in London, but her daydreams are filled with beaches and palm trees.

When she's not writing, you can find Kasia scouting out the best coffee shops in town, planning her next great adventure, or petting other people's puppies.

Anne Lown

Postal worker-turned-author, Anne Lown's career in the postal service, and her previous life in picturesque Devon, inevitably led to an interest in the small-town element of cozy mysteries. As she sorted the mail, she considered how evil can lurk behind the most delightful of settings.

Thankfully, she became an author, not a serial killer.

Anne has had the privilege of moderating the Facebook group for authors, 20Booksto50K, since 2018 and has delighted in cheering on fellow authors as their careers have grown and blossomed. She also runs the YouTube channel for the group.

Anne is the author of four novels and is working on the next in the current series, with others in development. At home, she is a life-long learner and hoarder of courses, much to the horror of her son. Her dog's interests are food and sleep.

Sìne Màiri MacDougall

Sìne Màiri is a Gàidhlig speaker from the Nova Scotian Gaidhealtachd. She's an author, international incident starter, and recovering educator. Having taught all over the world from the UK to Northern Canada to China, and back again, her specialties are language and literature, history, and youth services for alternative education. She unapologetically writes about the themes she's encountered in her travels; resilience and found family being chief amongst those themes.

Her current fiction projects include two urban fantasy series that she hopes to launch in the coming year.

Susan Odev

Susan has banked over three decades of work experience in the fields of personal and organizational development, being a freelance corporate trainer and consultant alongside holding down "real" jobs for over twenty-five years. Specializing in entrepreneurial mindsets, she has written several non-fiction business books, once gaining a coveted Amazon #1 best seller tag in business and entrepreneurship, an accolade she now strives to emulate with her fiction.

Currently working on her fifth novel, under a top secret pen name, the craft and marketing aspects of being a successful indie author equally fascinate and terrify her.

A lover of history with a criminal record collection, Susan lives in a retro orange and avocado world. Once described by a colleague as being an "onion," Susan has many layers, as have ogres (according to Shrek). She would like to think this makes her cool, her teenage children just think she's embarrassing.

Contributors

Fatima Fayez

As a contributing writer for Indie Author Magazine, Fatima unites her love of connecting with people and giving back to the author community. She is a co-founder of The Author Arena podcast, in addition to The Author Conference on Clubhouse. She is also an administrator for the 20BooksTo50K® Facebook group.

Fatima has lived in countries across Europe, Asia, and North America. During her various residencies, she managed to collect a bachelor of science in Journalism, along with a masters in Business Administration, and a handful of management certifications. She currently resides in Kuwait with her family.

On Saturdays, you can find her playing Dungeons & Dragons with her party.

Lasairiona McMaster

With a bachelor of arts in Politics and a minor in Culture and Media Studies, Lasairiona McMaster left the Emerald Isle for the great state of Texas and found her soul's home among queso and margaritas. When a decade of volunteering, expat and lifestyle blogging, and living abroad came to an end, she repatriated to Northern Ireland. Dusting off an old manuscript she'd penned in college, she hit the "publish" button in 2019, and hasn't looked back.

She writes relatable romance featuring themes of societal taboos, like male mental health, and that "just one book" is now a multi-series world that keeps growing.

When she's not in the writing cave, she's a professional nagger, developmental editor, and has mastered the art of making great friends from complete strangers. She's a left-handed Aquarian and enneagram four who loves to travel, sing, and never wears matching socks.

> Writing is an exploration. You start from nothing and learn as you go.
> E.L. Doctorow

Just typed
"The End"...

Is my website ready?

Build a stunning site

Wordpress Cohort

@ Indie Author
Tools University

writelink.to/iatu